52 Tips

for Texas Hold'em Poker

By Barry Shulman

with Mark Gregorich

Card Player Press

Las Vegas

ISBN 0-9758953-0-3

Published by **Card Player Press**
3140 S. Polaris Ave, Suite 8
Las Vegas, NV 89102
(702) 871-1720
www.CardPlayer.com

Edited by Michael Wiesenberg
Cover Design by Christy Devine
Interior Design by BJ Nemeth

Printed in the United States of America

Acknowledgments

I loved doing this book. For years I have dreamt of a really useful how-to book on hold'em that would be easy to grasp for beginners, yet sophisticated enough to help even the most advanced player.

It was particularly fun, as virtually the entire Card Player team worked on it.

"52 Tips for Texas Hold'em Poker" started as a spreadsheet of helpful hints for my wife, Allyn. She wanted specific how-tos not just the usual "it depends." Daily we went over the list to simplify and refine it. As the book was taking form she worked with me on every facet.

My list, however, was short, choppy, and really a list of guidelines more suited for verbal lessons. Mark Gregorich worked closely with me to recast the ideas into 52 specific tips.

Next, Michael Wiesenberg put the tips into clear, understandable, and proper English. Additionally he focused extensively on the development of a suitable glossary.

Christy Devine did the cover photo and orchestrated the entire look of the front and back cover. She was ably assisted by the Card Player creative department, including Jeremy Andrews, BJ Nemeth, and Brittney Burns, who all worked hard on the design and layout of the entire book.

Our administrative staff, headed by Dominik Karelus and Johnnie Walker, were active in creating the business of Card Player Press and actually getting the book published.

Finally, I want to acknowledge and thank my son Jeff, who is not only my constant sounding board, but oversees everything at Card Player, including this project.

CONTENTS

Introduction

Poker has had an explosion of growth in the 21st century. Poker has had booms in popularity before, particularly when hold'em was legalized in California in 1988. However, nothing in poker's history compares with what is happening now.

What's Behind the Growth?

Two factors have propelled poker to its current heights, and there doesn't look to be any limit to the growth.

First, today, you can watch poker on television almost every day of the year. The biggest success has been the phenomenal World Poker Tour, making superstars of tournament players. Network research has shown that poker has great "sticking power" among channel surfers: those who happen upon poker tend to continue to watch. Viewers see apparently ordinary people winning millions in tournaments and they become fascinated by this ultimate and yet most accessible of reality shows. This exposure has helped create an unprecedented interest in the game.

Second, while in the past people may have had the willingness to play poker, apart from weekly home games, most didn't have the opportunity. This is certainly no longer the case, however. Once confined in the United States to a few Western states, public cardrooms — some land-based, some on cruising or permanently docked riverboats, some full-blown casinos on Indian reservations — offering virtually nonstop poker games have spread to many states. Those states that don't have official cardrooms offer regular "charity nights" that include games for poker players. Twenty years ago poker was available in the

United States and the United Kingdom, and that was about it. Now, the casinos of many European countries, as well as Canada, Australia, and countries in Central and South America, offer poker. And, even if a live poker game is not available in your area, the advent of Internet poker allows you to play from the comfort of your own home. In fact, Internet poker has largely contributed to poker's recent exponential growth.

Not All Forms of Poker Have Benefited Equally

While it is true that more people than ever are playing poker today, not all of the many forms of the game have benefited equally from its popularity explosion. In fact, you could argue that poker's growth has in reality been specific to only one form of the game — Texas hold'em*. Everyone seems to want to play hold'em today, whether it's the no-limit version seen on television and played primarily in tournaments, or the limit version that constitutes most of the games in public cardrooms and on the Internet. Even many "Saturday night" types of players, who for years have enjoyed their creative kitchen-table forms of poker, now are switching to hold'em.

The Golden Age of Hold'em

This is truly the Golden Age of hold'em. If there is one form of poker to learn or to specialize in, it's hold'em. Not only will you find more games to choose from, but the players in these games tend to be less knowledgeable and experienced than those in other forms of poker, like seven-card stud. Simply put, hold'em games should be easier to beat than other games just because that's what everyone is playing.

In poker, your results over time are based on the quality of your play relative to your opposition. This explains why a player may be able to win at the games at a particular limit, but not at a higher limit — the quality of opposition tends to increase as you progress in limits (although this is not always true). With the huge influx of new hold'em players, you will be playing against a large number of inexperienced, less-skilled players. Thus, hold'em games often are very lucrative.

---

* Although the "official" name of the game is Texas hold'em, almost everyone shortens that to just hold'em. We're going to do that in the rest of this book.

Being capable of making money at hold'em assumes, of course, that you play better than your opponents. Unfortunately, this won't happen overnight, and although it is certainly possible to walk into a cardroom, sit right down, and win on your very first session, it's just not very likely. The large amount of short-term luck in poker makes it possible for anyone to be a winner on any particular day, but if you plan on playing more than once it's not a bad idea to know what you're doing.

The Paradox of Hold'em

One of the fascinating aspects about hold'em is its dual nature. The game is both incredibly simple and incredibly complex. If you've watched any World Poker Tour (WPT) broadcast, you've heard hold'em described as a game that "takes a minute to learn and a lifetime to master." That is really true, and a large part of the appeal of the game is that you can sit down and learn how to play almost immediately. In this sense, hold'em can be approached like other games found in a casino, where you can understand the basic mechanics of the game well enough to play it, and the luck element presents you with some chance of emerging a winner.

However, after playing a bit, you become aware that hold'em has many layers, each more complex than the previous one. The deeper you develop your understanding of the game, the better your results should be. The best thing for you is this: most players never work to develop their games. What they know about the game is strictly what they draw from their personal experience at the table, much of which they don't properly interpret. In fact they often misinterpret their experience in counterproductive ways. So there is great opportunity for those who wish to invest a bit of time and effort in improving their game.

Tools for Today's Hold'em Players

Modern hold'em players have many tools to assist in shortening the learning time. There are videos, computer software, seminars, Internet chat forums, personal poker trainers for hire, and, of course, books. Currently, a huge number of books on limit hold'em are available, with many more being written. However, very little exists for the brand new player, whose only exposure to hold'em may be what he has seen on television and perhaps a few hands played at a casino or in a home game.

Why You Need this Book

This book provides someone who has played little or no limit hold'em with a sound basic strategy that will add to both his enjoyment of the game and his bottom line. You must walk before you can run, and this book teaches those first steps.

How to Use this Book

If you absorb and put into practice the information in this book, you should become a winning low-limit hold'em player. This will put you ahead of the 90 percent or so of public cardroom poker players who lose money at the game. Once you acquire a framework for beating the game, you can then take your game to the next level.

The book is designed for simplicity. We present 52 tips, each of which provides a valuable kernel of information. We present the tips chronologically as you progress through a hand of hold'em. Obviously, everything to know about hold'em cannot be reduced to just 52 items. However, these 52 tips deal with some of the most important and most frequently encountered decisions you will have to make.

Hold'em can be both very complex and quite simple. This book keeps the game as simple as possible for you. Specifically, we do this by presenting a strategy that helps you steer clear of many of the common pitfalls in hold'em, pitfalls that can quickly erode your stack of chips. Staying out of potentially dangerous situations is very important to a player new to the game, as many of them require a feel for the game that only experience can produce.

Although this book is aimed at the newer player, the concepts are relevant to all levels of hold'em. Thus, we think that most players will find some benefits to their game by reading this book. Even if the tips presented in the book are not new to you, you will find it beneficial to treat them as a refresher course, since a true mastery of poker involves not only learning concepts, but remembering and putting them into practice.

Tip Order

The 52 tips presented in this book appear in approximately chronological order. That is, after the first three tips, we start with play prior to the flop, then on the flop, and so on.

How To Play Hold'em

This section is for those who have not played hold'em before. It describes how to play a hand.

The Deal

Years ago players in all games dealt for themselves. The deal rotated clockwise (one position to the left) after each hand. Nowadays, most cardrooms have house dealers who deal all the cards, maintain table decorum, ensure the pots and betting are correct, see that players act in turn, and award pots to the winning players. The position from which the dealer would distribute cards if the dealer were one of the players is indicated by a *dealer button*. Most players call it simply *the button*. The button is often a white disk approximately the size of a hockey puck, sometimes labeled "button." From now on, when we speak of the button, we will be referring either to that disk or to the player who sits in that position. You'll be able to tell by context what we mean.

When the house dealer distributes cards to the players, he always starts with the player in the seat to the left of the button and ends with the button.

All online cardrooms use a button, and it is a graphical representation of the preceding.

Antes and Blinds

Also in those old days, back when the main game in cardrooms was five-card draw, players put *antes* into each pot. An ante is a payment made by each player to the pot prior to receiving cards. An ante is not a bet because it does not "play for" the player. The purpose of the antes is to stimulate action. Without money in the pot, the first player would never have an incentive to open the betting because there would be nothing to win.

Antes are still used in forms of seven-card stud and they also appear in the later stages of no-limit hold'em tournaments. Generally, though, hold'em-type games use *blinds*. Blinds serve the same purpose as antes, to stimulate action. Unlike an ante, however, a blind is considered to be a bet made before the cards are dealt, and it "plays for" the player. That is, an amount equal to the size of the blind is part of a player's bet later on.

Usually, the player to the immediate left of the button puts chips into the pot equal to half the size of the lower limit of the game. Those chips (and the player who puts the chips in) are called the *small blind*. The next player to the left, that is, the player two positions to the left of the button, puts chips into the pot equal to size of the limit of the game. Those chips (and the player who puts the chips in) are called the *big blind*. For example, if the stakes are $4-$8 — this would be called a $4-$8 limit game — the small blind is $2 and the big blind is $4.

First Round

The dealer distributes first one card face down to each player, starting with the small blind, and then another. The cards are always dealt clockwise in any poker game. When each player has two *hole cards,* as they are called, the deal stops and the *action* begins. Here action means betting, raising, and folding.

Hold'em has four rounds of betting.

On the first round of betting, the action commences with the player immediately to the left of the big blind. Just as in the deal rotation and the distribution of cards, the action in any poker game always proceeds clockwise. The first player has three options. Let's use the $4-$8 game as our example. He can fold his hand (choose not to play and relinquish his cards to the dealer), call $4, or raise by putting $8 into the pot. In limit hold'em, the increments of all bets and raises are determined by the limits of the game. On the first two betting rounds, bets and raises are in increments of the lower limit; on the last two betting rounds, bets and raises are in increments of the higher limit. If the first player folds, each succeeding player has the same options.

If the first player opens for the minimum, that is, does not raise, each succeeding player can fold, call (by matching the opening bet), or raise, by putting $8 into the pot.

Opening for the minimum has a special term. It is called *limping.*

If the first player comes in for a raise, that is, initiates the betting by putting $8 into the pot, succeeding players must fold, call the new amount, or raise by an additional $4.

The Cap

Limit games have another limit that comes into play, and that is a limit on the number of raises *in any one round.* Some cardrooms permit one bet and three raises in any one round. Other cardrooms permit one bet and four raises in any one round. The total number of bets permitted is called the *cap;* that last bet is also called the cap. Players use the word as a verb, also, when they say, "The betting was capped." You want to find out what the cap is before you start playing. You can ask the house dealer when you first sit down, if you wish, although if you don't want to be immediately pegged as a "newbie," you might ask a floorman before you sit down.

Betting by the Blinds

On the first round of betting, the blinds act after everyone else. After the button has folded, opened or called (as appropriate), or raised, the small blind acts. Since the small blind already has chips in the pot, if he plays he adds only as much to the pot as to make the total equal the bet. In our example of the $4-$8 game, we saw that the small blind has $2 that plays for him in the pot. If players have limped and there have been no raises, he can participate by adding $2 to the pot. Just as any other player, the small blind can fold, call, or raise. If everyone has folded *except* the small blind, the small blind has those same three options. If anyone has raised before the action gets to the small blind, he can get in for $2 less. For example, if there has been one raise, the total bet would be $8. The small blind can play by adding $6 to the pot — or reraise by adding $10.

The big blind is the last to act on the first round of betting. If one or more players have called the initial bet — that is, if the players have all limped — the big blind has two choices. This situation is called the *option*. He can elect to simply check. This effectively ends the betting for the round. However, the big blind has another choice when the action gets to him with no raises. Even though he has already technically made a bet — the big blind, after all, is a bet — and there has been no raise, he can himself raise. In a *brick-and-mortar cardroom*, when the action gets to the big blind without anyone having raised, the house dealer usually says something like "Your option" or "Option." Sometimes the dealer just points at the player. In an online cardroom, when the action similarly gets to the big blind, the software presents two choices, one prompting "raise" and the other "check." The effect is the same.

If, however, there has been a raise, the big blind now must either match the raise (call), raise the pot himself, or fold his hand.

The Flop
After the action is complete for the first round, that is, at the point that all the betting has been equalized, the dealer places three cards face up in the center of the table. This is called the *flop*. These cards are called *community cards,* and each player uses them in combination with his own two cards. Each player tries to form the best five-card hand from some combination of his two hole cards and the five community cards.

Because community cards are part of every player's hand, a flop of A-A-A is ordinarily nothing to get too excited about. Yes, you have three aces, but so do all your opponents. If you have the remaining ace in your hand, however, some inner rejoicing may be appropriate.

A second round of betting now begins. This time the betting starts with the first *active player* to the dealer's left. (An active player is one who has met all the betting thus far.) The first round of betting is the only one in which the betting does not start immediately to the left of the button — and that is because of the blinds. The first player has two options. He can *check* (make no bet but retain his cards) or bet. Only in the first round must each player in turn bet or fold until a bet has been made — also because of the blinds. If someone bets on the second round, each remaining player has three options: fold, call (equal the preceding bet), or raise. The action continues around the table until the betting for that round has been equalized — with the same proviso about the cap as on the first round.

The Turn

The dealer places a fourth card face up in the center of the table, adjacent to the three flop cards. This card is called the *turn*. Another round of betting follows, only this time, the stakes double. In a $4-$8 game, the first two rounds of betting are in $4 increments. On the turn, betting occurs in $8 increments. Apart from that, players have the same betting options as the previous round. They can check or bet if no bet has yet been made. They can fold, call, or raise if a bet has been made — up to the cap.

The River

Finally, the dealer places the fifth card face up in the center of the table, adjacent to the four community cards already there. This card is known as the *river*. A final round of betting takes place, again at the higher level.

When the betting has been equalized, there is a *showdown* of all remaining hands, and the best hand wins the pot.

If only one player remains; that is, there has been a bet or raise that has not been called, then that player wins the pot and no cards are shown. The exception is if any player is *all in*, that is, has run out of chips, there still is a showdown, even though the betting has not been equalized. You can never be bet out of a pot just because you run out of chips before a hand is over. If you run out of chips and other players have chips left with which to bet, then a *side pot* is created that the all-in player cannot win. On the showdown, the best hand in contention for the main pot wins it, and the best hand in contention for the side pot wins that. The same hand might win both the main pot and side pot.

Reading the Board

If you are new to hold'em, one of your top priorities should be to learn how to accurately *read the board* (how the community cards relate to your two cards). Reading the board in hold'em is not nearly as complex as in games such as Omaha eight-or-better.

It's important, nonetheless. These examples show situations that beginners sometimes misread.

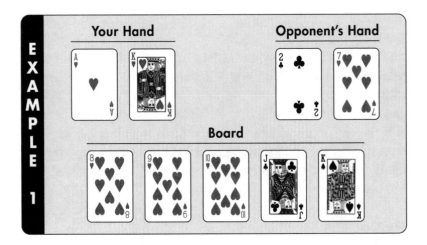

In Example 1, your hand is the ace-high (*nut**) flush, which beats your opponent's hand. He uses his 7♡ with the 8♡ 9♡ T♡ J♣ on the board to make a straight. If either the 6♡ or J♡ had been the river card, instead of the K♣, your opponent would have a straight flush — and win. When you start with considerably the best of it, such as this situation of flopping the nut flush, and end up losing on the river to a straight flush against a player who starts with only one card of that suit, you have suffered what players call a *bad beat*. Part of the ability to read the board should include realizing that even if you have the nut flush, if three — or four! — cards to a straight flush are on the board, you might end up losing. And it will be costly if you do. So if a *solid* (conservative, not likely to get out of line) opponent keeps raising on the turn or the river in a situation in which you think you have the nuts, take another look at the board to see if a better hand is possible.

Who wins the hand in Example 2? Although you have two pair, you lose the pot to your opponent's A-K. Why? He can play sevens and fours with an ace kicker, while you must *play the board*. That is, the best hand you can make by using the best five of the seven

---

* *Nut* refers to the best possible hand for the situation. Thus a *nut flush* is the best possible flush that can be made. With four hearts on the board, for example, whoever holds the A♡ has the nut flush. Similarly, with a board of 6♡ 7◇ 8◇ Q♡ A♣, anyone with hole cards T-9 of any suits would have the *nut straight*. That hand would also be known as *the nuts*, because it is the best possible hand that can be made with that board.

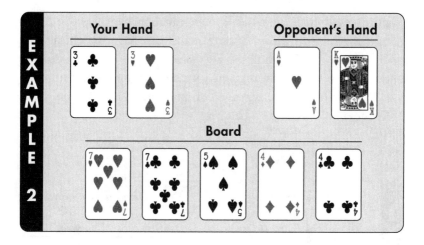

available to you is what's on the board, sevens and fours with a 5 kicker. Your pair of threes have been *counterfeited* by the appearance of a second pair, higher than yours, on the board. You had the best hand right up to the river, and would have won the pot if the river card had been any 2, 3, 6, 7, 8, 9, T*, J, or Q. Of the 44 cards left in the deck at the turn, 32 would have made you a winner. You got unlucky when the river card was not one of those.

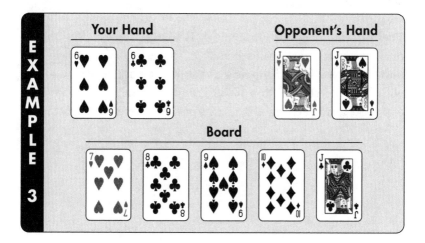

The hand illustrated in Example 3 is a split pot. Both you and your opponent have a jack-high straight. In fact, neither one of you

---

* T: 10.

is playing either of your two cards. Your opponent had the better hand on the turn with an already made jack-high straight against your 10-high straight, but the jack on the river counterfeited his hand. On the turn, there remained in the deck only two cards that would cause him not to win the pot, and one of those came. That, too, would be considered a bad beat.

Notice that if a third opponent was in the hand holding a queen, he would win the pot.

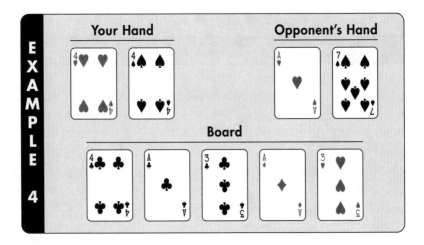

The A-7 wins the pot in Example 4. His hand is aces full of threes, playing only the ace in his hand. You have fours full of aces, the same hand you had on the turn. If you lose a pot this way (and you will), you are entitled to a bit of grumbling. And notice that your opponent would also have won if an ace or 7 came on the river.

Three Universal Hold'em Concepts

Three points about hold'em are universal, and so we present them first. You must always keep these in mind, at every stage of the hand. These are:

- your playing style: some ways of playing are profitable, while others are not
- the great importance of position in hold'em
- the significance that pot odds have on your decisions

The first three tips deal with these universal concepts.

Tip 1

A tight-aggressive playing style gets the money in hold'em.

Adopting a *tight-aggressive* playing style is a winning strategy in *all* forms of poker. You would have a hard time finding a poker game in which this is not the case. To play a winning game of hold'em, you should (and must) adopt this style of play.

How do we define "tight-aggressive"?

Tight means entering fewer pots than most of your opponents. Being selective by playing only quality starting hands is the key here. "Quality starting hands" is a relative term — sometimes hands that are good in one situation are quite weak in another, and vice versa. As this book progresses, you will learn to read *situations* and how your read influences which hands are playable, and which are not.

Aggressive means that when you do decide to enter a pot, you play the hand for all it's worth. You place an emphasis on betting, raising, and check-raising. Checking and calling just does not get the job done most of the time. There are some situations in which this is the correct play (and the text will identify these situations for you), but they are the exception. By the way, an aggressive approach does not mean that once you decide to play a hand, you jam your foot on the gas pedal and don't ease up until the pot has been played out. Like most things in life, hold'em requires discretion, and that will come from experience.

How the World Poker Tour Has Affected Poker Play

One by-product of the recent popularity of the World Poker Tour (WPT) is that a whole new breed of poker player has been created. If you watch the show with your goal being to learn how to be a world-class poker player, you may be in for a rude awakening when you go to play. The problems with using the show as a learning device for live game limit hold'em are numerous. Right away, realize that you are watching a different poker game. It may *look* the same; after all, the players are dealt two cards, and there are blinds, flops, turns, and rivers. That is where the similarities end, though. What you are witnessing is the end of a no-limit tournament, in which the blinds are high, the game is shorthanded, and the program has been edited to showcase the more interesting hands. This book talks about limit hold'em, which plays completely differently from the no-limit game. Also, when you play in a brick-and-mortar cardroom or online, unless you are in a tournament, the blinds are not large compared to your stack size. You are probably in a nine- or ten-handed game. And you see all of the hands dealt, not just those that some producer thinks might turn out to be interesting.

Loose-aggressive play seems to be a winning style on the WPT. The successful players are in there dancing around with hands that you toss into the muck without a second thought. And the thing is, they are correct (most of the time) to play these hands, and you are correct to throw them away. The reason for this is that we are dealing with totally different circumstances.

As a newer player who has not yet developed a good understanding of the game, you may think it self-evident to emulate the style of play you witness on television. After all, if T-2 is good enough for a world-class player, it should be good enough for you. So, as a new "television era" player, you may enter the game playing an extremely loose-aggressive style, and believe that to be a winning strategy. In reality, what you are doing is playing final table no-limit short-handed poker in a full limit hold'em game. You will not win playing like this, unless your opponents are all doing the same (only doing it worse).

The Tight-Aggressive Edge

So, how exactly does a tight-aggressive approach give you an edge over your opponents? If you have played much low-limit hold'em, you have probably found the games typically to be loose (with four or more opponents seeing the flop on average), and for many hands to go to the showdown. This means that to win you must show the best hand most of the time, as bluffing is difficult in these games (one more down side to being a TV student).

The *tight* part of tight-aggressive means that you play fewer hands than your average opponent. Thus, it stands to reason that the quality of your starting cards is typically higher than those of other players, which in turn means that a higher percentage of the hands you play reach the showdown as the best hand. Since bluffing is typically not a viable option in loose low-limit games, playing hands that often end up at the river as the best hand is obviously a desirable strategy. This book teaches you which hands are worth playing and which are not, based on the situation.

By playing good cards aggressively, you win the maximum amount from your winning hands. If your opponents wish to stay in the pot against you with inferior cards, you should charge them as much as possible to do so. An added benefit of aggressive play (and a key one) is that you will win some pots that your more passive playing opponents do not, by inducing opponents to fold hands that ultimately would have won the pot. You can't win these "default pots" by checking and calling.

Tip 2

*Hold'em is
a game of
position.*

In poker, *position* refers to when a player must act on his hand relative to the other players in the pot. When a player is one of the first to act, he is in *early position*. When a player is last or nearly last, he is in *late position*. Similarly, players with several opponents on either side of them are in *middle position*. These terms appear frequently in this book, which provides a clue about the significance of considering position in your hold'em decisions.

Late Position Advantage

As you begin to play hold'em, you quickly become aware of the numerous advantages of having late position in a hand.

One of the most important advantages is that you generally have a decent idea of what kind of strength you are up against. For example, suppose you are holding 8-8. This looks like a good hand, and, in absolute terms, it is just that. It is not, however, a *great* hand, and it is often unclear how (or whether) to proceed with it.

If you are in late position with your pocket eights, the actions of the other players influence how you play. Suppose everyone has folded to you, and only the blinds are yet to act. It is highly probable that you have the best hand, so you should choose to play it aggressively by raising the pot. Assuming the blinds call your raise, you now hold a positional advantage over them for the remainder of the hand. This means that on the flop, turn, and river, they must act before you, giving you the advantage of making your decisions with more information about your opponents' cards than they have about yours.

Let's look at a different scenario in which you hold 8-8 in late position. This time, however, a tight player has raised and an even tighter one has reraised before the action has reached you. Once again, the useful information gained due to your positional advantage can be used. Clearly, your two eights are not the best hand here, and this knowledge, combined with the high price of entering the pot, allows you to safely fold your hand.

Early Position Disadvantage
Contrast this with holding the same hand in early position. Poker is a game of incomplete information, and the earlier your position, the more incomplete the information. Now, you don't have the benefit of knowing what your opponents are going to do. You must make a poorly informed decision, and in poker these kinds of decisions are often wrong. In the case of the 8-8, sometimes it is the best hand (or at least playable), and other times it is way behind. Thus, the earlier your position, the less likely you are to know which one is the case.

But the problems with early position don't stop there. Once you decide to enter a pot by opening early (or decide to look at the flop from a blind position), you act before your middle and late position opponents for the remainder of the hand. This will cost you, in terms of both bets and pots. Because you must act first, you will at times be unsure as to whether a card helped your opponents' hands. For example, you may check, when in fact had you bet your hand one or more opponents might have called with inferior hands. Your poor position has cost you one or more bets in this case.

Worse yet, your apprehension about whether the development of the board has helped your opponents may cause you to check, when betting would have induced everyone else to fold. Now, suppose everyone checks behind you, and the next card comes. An opponent who would have folded for a bet on the previous betting round now improves his hand and wins the pot. For example, suppose you are first to act with 8-8, and the flop is K-9-7. If you are first, with three or four players behind you, you would probably choose (correctly) to check, as this flop is likely to have helped one or more of your opponents. However, suppose nobody can beat your pair of eights, and the hand gets checked around. Now, an ace comes, giving one of your opponents holding A-5 a better hand. Since this player would probably have folded on the flop had you bet, your check has cost you the pot. If you had the same hand in last position, however, it would have been correct for you to bet the flop once it was checked around to you, likely making you the winner of the pot.

Playing Position

Clearly, it is to your benefit to try to play most of your hands from late position. As a result, you should enter the pot only with premium hands when you are one of the first players to act. When you play only big pairs and big cards such as A-K from early position, your postflop positional disadvantage is partially offset by your hand being fairly easy to play after the flop. If you have a big pair, you stay aggressive on the flop in nearly all cases (the main exception being when your pair is smaller than aces, an ace flops, and several players are in the pot). If you have big cards, such as A-K, you tend to bet when you flop a pair, and check when you don't (tempered by certain factors to be discussed later). These hands don't require as much guesswork; thus, their postflop performance does not suffer as much from poor position as do more marginal holdings like small and middle pairs.

Because you have the benefit of observing the actions of all your opponents, you can be much more liberal with your starting requirements when you are in late position. Don't misinterpret "liberal" as "loose" or "sloppy," though. Some hands are not profitable to play in *any* situation. Nevertheless, acting last allows you, first, to see how your hand figures to stack up against your opponents before the flop, and, then, to make well-informed decisions about how to proceed after the flop.

Do not underestimate the value of position. It should be a consideration in nearly every decision you make in the game.

Tip 3

Be aware of pot odds at all times.

Pot odds is another important poker concept, with applications throughout the play of a hand. Essentially, pot odds refers to how the amount of money in the pot influences your decision to play or pass. For those of you new to this concept, here is an example to help clarify. Suppose you are holding K-Q, and see a flop of 3-T-J. As you can see, any ace or 9 will make you the nut straight. Also, a king or queen pairs you, which may or may not produce a winning hand. You can determine your pot odds if you know the following:

- how much money is in the pot
- how much it will cost you to stay in the hand
- what your chances are of making the best hand

For this example, let's say that there is $100 in the pot, and it costs you $10 to call a bet. Also, for simplicity's sake, assume that we are talking only about making your hand on the next card, and that you will win only if you make a straight.

You can express your likelihood of making the best hand by forming a ratio of the cards that miss you to the cards that make your hand. In this case, that would be 39-to-8. (This representation is called *odds*.) Of the 47 unseen cards, 39 are *blanks* (cards that do not make your hand), while eight (the four nines and four aces) make you a straight. You can also express this same relationship as a fraction, 8/47, or a shade better than 1 in 6. (This representation is called *chances*.)

Here, the difference between odds and chances is that odds usually refer to the *unlikelihood* of an event (like making a hand) and chances usually refer to the *likelihood* of the event. Odds are expressed as a *ratio*, with the larger number being the ways of missing and the smaller number the ways of hitting. In our example, there are 39 ways of missing the straight and eight of making it. Thus, the *odds against* making the straight are 39-to-8. Chances are expressed as a *fraction*, with the denominator being the *total number of possibilities* and the numerator the ways of hitting. In our example, there are 47 possible outcomes, of which eight make the hand. Thus, the *chances* of making the straight are 8/47.

Now, it is time to combine those three points above to determine the correct course of action. It is wrong to automatically call with your hand simply because you have a straight draw. You must make sure that the pot is offering you the proper odds (the *right price*) to call.

You can express the price the pot is offering you as both a ratio (in this case, it is 100-to-10); and as a fraction (10/110). Reduced, you are getting pot odds of 10-to-1 on your call. What this means is that as long as you will make your hand more than one time in 11, it is profitable for you to draw. Since your chances of improving your K-Q to a straight are about 1 in 6, calling is clearly the right play.

What about an inside straight draw? With this holding, you have only four ways to make a straight. This makes your chances 4/47, or just slightly better than 1 in 12. With the same size pot and cost to call, a fold is now in order, since you will not make your hand often enough for drawing at it to be profitable. Had either the pot been larger or the amount of the bet smaller, however, calling often would be correct.

How Much Math Do You Need?

So, do you have to be a math wiz to play hold'em? Absolutely not! Poker at its essence is a game of people and logical thought. The ability to do complex mathematical equations in your head, while impressive, will probably not be of much benefit to you here.

You should, however, have a good working knowledge of odds and probability. Whether you do this in your head on the spot, or take some time to learn by rote the odds of making certain draws, you should not neglect this aspect of the game. Failure to learn the odds may cause you not only to call when you should fold, but also to fold when you should be calling. It is perfectly acceptable to memorize a chart showing the odds of completing the various draws. Doing so will save you from having to make on-the-spot calculations. (You can find an odds chart for various poker draws in the Appendix, on page 149.)

In many cases, your decision whether to pursue a draw is quite obvious. For example, suppose you must pay $10 to draw to a flush (nine cards make the hand) when there is $300 in the pot. The pot offers 30-to-1 and the odds against making your hand are only 38-to-9 (a little worse than 4-to-1). In a situation like this, your hand plays fairly automatically. However, situations frequently arise in which your continued involvement in the pot is questionable, due to the close alignment between the cost of remaining in the hand, the size of the pot, and the odds against making your draw. For example, if you must call $20 to win $60, and the odds against making your hand are 3-to-1, it is a virtual dead heat. Mathematically, it doesn't matter whether you call or fold. It's a break-even proposition either way.

There are many close, "coin flip" type decisions in poker, in which it doesn't appear to matter which decision you make. However, good poker players learn to include additional factors in their analysis of a hand. Decisions that at first appear to be cases of "six of one, half a dozen of the other" become clear-cut after further study. But, that is what the rest of this book is about.

Playing Before the Flop

The most important decision you make during a hand of hold'em is whether to enter the pot in the first place. As a winning player, your greatest single source of profit comes from those who play hands they should be folding. The mistake of entering a pot with a marginal or inferior hand can easily be compounded by improving the hand just enough on the flop to continue with it until the end. For example, hands such as 8-6 *offsuit* (not suited, that is, of different suits) should rarely, if ever, be played, for the reason that even when they improve (by flopping a pair or a straight draw), they often don't win the pot. In this manner, an initial mistake of playing a bad hand has paved the way for the rest of the hand, which could turn out to be quite expensive.

The tips in this section help you avoid this trap, by showing a tight-aggressive approach to hand selection. We can't possibly cover every possible situation, but we hope that the use of numerous examples is effective in forming general guidelines in your mind as to how to play hold'em before the flop.

Note: This section contains statements like "raise with a pair of jacks." Interpret that to mean that raising in the situation under discussion is correct when you are holding any hand equal to *or better than* a pair of jacks. Similar statements appear regarding the play of unpaired cards and cards that are *suited* (of the same suit). For example, if you see "raise with A-J," of course that means that if you have A-Q you also raise.

Tip 4

Raise or fold when you are first to enter a pot.

This tip refers to those situations in which no one has yet called or raised when the action gets to you.

Since tight-aggressive poker is winning poker, you should fold your inferior hands. Don't call trying to hit a lucky flop. Not only is it tough to get a nice flop when you are holding *rags* (substandard cards), but if you initiate the action by calling, this is often seen as an invitation for other players to call behind you. Now, you must play an inferior hand while out of position. This is not a winning proposition.

When you do have a good hand, you should open the pot with a raise. In addition to putting pressure on the players yet to act and the blinds, your raise allows you to take the lead in the pot. Even if you miss the flop completely, a bet on the flop, coupled with the strength you demonstrated with your initial raise, may be enough to win the pot.

Generally, it is advisable to open the pot only if you feel your hand is likely to be the best. This means that hands such as 8-7 suited, while playable in some cases, should not be played when you are first in. This hand is not strong enough to merit a raise, and calling when first in is not in your repertoire. If you are unsure of whether your hand is worthy of a raise, a good guideline for playing before the flop is that whenever you are in doubt, you should fold. You will be dealt plenty of hands with which you can forge ahead aggressively.

5 ♠

Tip 5

Your position is of vital importance in deciding whether to open the pot.

♥ 5

As detailed earlier, you should strive to play most of your hands from late position, since this allows you to ascertain more accurately the strength of your opponents. At no point in the hand is this more evident than in deciding whether to open a pot for a raise.

Very few hands should be played from early position, which can be classified as the first three seats in a 10-handed game. You won't go wrong sticking to only premium hands, such as J-J, A-K, or A-Q suited. In good games (those with several weak players), money can be made by playing T-T, 9-9, A-J, and K-Q suited as well. This is because the poorer players will be calling your raises with worse hands than these, which would not necessarily be the case in tighter games.

If the other players have folded to you and you are sitting in any middle position, you can add a few more hands to your opening range. Now, pairs such as 9-9 are definitely worth a raise, as are big suited cards such as A-J or K-Q. A-Q offsuit is also worth raising now. The hands 8-8, A-T suited, and A-J offsuit are marginal here, becoming more playable in later middle position.

On the button, you can dramatically expand your playbook when it's folded to you. The primary reason for this is that you have only the blinds to contend with, meaning that even if they should decide to *defend* (call from a blind position in a raised pot), you will hold position on them for the remainder of the hand. Pairs such as 5-5 should be played in virtually every situation, and you can raise with the baby pairs too, if the blinds are *either* very tight or poor players. You want to capitalize on players who play too tight in the blinds by raising them at every opportunity. When a poor player is in the blind and you hold the button, you shouldn't mind playing quite a variety of hands either, as you hold position on this inferior player for the rest of the hand. This is a good way to attract chips your way.

In addition to any pair, you can open on the button with hands as weak as K-T or Q-T offsuit, or with suited hands such as K-8. The button is the one time you may wish to open with a drawing hand. Again, position is a major reason, along with the fact that if both blinds fold, you win the pot right away. Even if you do get called, your position and aggression will often allow you to pick up the pot with a bet on the flop.

Tip 6

When one or more players have called in front of you, you need a big hand to raise.

Although you would prefer to get some action when you pick up a *monster* (an extremely good hand for a particular situation) such as A-A or K-K, one of the incentives for raising when you enter a pot is the possibility that you may simply win the blinds right away. However, this is not the case when one or more players have entered the pot before the action gets to you. Since other players have shown a willingness to compete for the pot, you need a very good hand to raise.

Some knowledge of your opponents comes in handy here. If you pay attention when you sit in a game to what types of hands your opponents are turning over, you learn their starting requirements. (Also observe their position when they enter a pot.) You may not even need to see their hands; if a player calls 80 percent of the hands before the flop, he is likely to show you just about anything. Conversely, alarm bells should sound in your head if another player enters his first hand since you sat down — hours ago. These types of playing styles definitely influence whether some of your hands merit a raise.

In general, when a typical player has called in front of you, you need a hand such as J-J, A-K, or A-Q suited to raise. When several players are in, you should elevate your standards even more. Raise with Q-Q or A-K suited. If one loose player has called, you can raise with some additional hands, such as 9-9, A-Q, or K-Q suited. If the one caller is exceptionally solid, these hands are only worth a call, however, and raises should be limited to J-J, A-K, or A-Q suited.

Tip 7

When players have already entered the pot for one bet, there are some playable hands that are worth a call but not a raise, because they need to improve to win the pot.

♥
7

As in Tip 6, some hands are profitable to play, but don't have to be played for a raise. This may seem to contradict the tight-aggressive style being preached here. However, this is not necessarily the case. When you make a raise in hold'em, you should have a clear objective. Essentially, raises are made for one of two reasons. The first is to eliminate players, and the second is to increase the size of the pot due to the strength of your hand.

When players have already called the initial bet, your raise will not accomplish the first objective. It may cut down on the number of *additional* players to enter the hand, but if several players have already called, you will still be facing a multiway situation. Thus, should you choose to raise, you are not doing it for the purpose of eliminating players.

So, with players already in the pot, the main reason for you to raise is to increase the size of the pot due to the strength of your hand. Few hands are strong enough to merit a raise here. These hands are summarized in Tip 6.

Calling is correct with hands that play well against several players. Primarily, these hands include medium pairs from fives to tens, and big suited cards such as K-Q or A-J. The reason why you don't raise with these hands is that they need improvement to win. For the big suited cards, you need to flop a pair, straight draw, or flush draw to continue with the hand. For the pairs, you need to flop a *set* (three of a kind), although flops such as 2-2-5 are frequently good enough for a hand such as 9-9 when four or five players are in the pot. So, by just calling preflop, you are able to make a minimal initial investment, allowing you to release your hand quickly and painlessly when the flop misses you. However, should you catch a nice flop, you can now go into an offensive mode. Essentially, with these types of hands in multiway situations, you are saving your tight-aggressive play until *after* the flop, when you have more information.

Sometimes you are sitting in late position holding a decent hand when five or more players have limped in. How should these *family pots* (those with multiple players) affect your starting requirements? First, remember that with so many participants, it will likely require a better than normal hand to end up winning the pot. In two- or three-way pots, hands such as *top pair* (one of your cards matching the highest card on the board, such as A-9 and a flop of 9-4-2) tend to get the job done. However, top pair (even two aces) will usually not be enough against more than five opponents.

So, you should look to play hands that have the potential to develop beyond just one pair. Hands such as A-T offsuit are virtually worthless in these situations, as they contain little straight or flush potential. Instead, good hands include any pair and big connecting suited cards. With a pair, you should win a nice pot if you flop a set, as one of your many opponents will likely pay you off when he holds top pair. The hand T-9 suited is definitely playable here, as it possesses the versatility of turning into a straight or a flush. However, with a hand such as this, you can't get too excited when you flop a pair, if several players are involved. You will likely be either *outkicked** or outdrawn, as a middle pair is extremely vulnerable.

---

* Outkicked: Losing with a pair because an opponent has the same pair, but with a higher kicker (side card). For example, you have J-T and the board is J-9-6-3-2. If you lose to a player with A-J, you have been *outkicked*.

Tip 8

8 ♠

When one player has raised, and it has been folded around to you, you should stick to the raise-or-fold philosophy.

♥ 8

Following this advice will keep you out of trouble. Many hold'em hands seem like they should be worth seeing the flop, but when you look at the situation objectively, you see that these hands just get you into trouble.

For example, suppose a player has raised from early position, and you have A-J. At first glance, this seems like a good hand. After all, you have two high cards including an ace. However, when you consider the range of hands the raiser is likely to hold, your A-J doesn't seem so mighty. (The assumption here is that the raiser only raises with decent hands.) It is very important to think about what sorts of hands your various opponents are capable of raising with, and from what positions.

When you think this way, you see that getting involved in a raised pot (when the raiser is a typical player from early position) with A-J is not a profitable strategy. In all likelihood, the raiser is holding one of two hands: a medium or high pair, or two high cards including an ace. If it's the first possibility, his pair is probably in the range of aces down to eights. So, if you have A-J, you are in decent shape against eights, nines, or tens. However, you are a sizable underdog against jacks, queens, or kings, and a monster underdog should you be unlucky enough to run into two aces. That is, more than half the pair hands he is likely to have put you at a severe disadvantage. Against two big cards with an ace, you are approximately a 5-to-2 underdog if they are A-K or A-Q. You are a favorite against A-T, but many opponents won't raise with this hand. If your opponent is almost certain to have either a pair or ace-something here — and that "something" is almost sure to be a high card — he'll have a hand with an ace in it more than half the time. Thus, overall, you're likely to be severely behind something over three-fourths of the time. So, although your A-J looks like a good enough hand (particularly if you've spent the better part of the last hour looking at 9-2 and 8-4), if you play it here you're asking for trouble. So, fold your hand and wait for a better situation.

With a hand that figures to be the best, it is good to reraise and make things tough on the players yet to act. Against one early-position raiser, if you stick to a general philosophy of reraising with J-J or better or with A-K, and folding all other hands, you will tend to get involved mostly in situations in which you are holding the better hand. And, if you consistently start with the best hand, you should do just fine in the game.

However, when the pot is opened by a raise from a late position player, the situation changes considerably. It is helpful to possess some knowledge of your opponents' playing styles here. Some players feel that "any two will do" when the hand has been folded around to them in late position. So they raise, attempting either to steal the blinds or play against them with position. When confronted with a player like this, you must expand the range of hands with which you are willing to go to battle. Otherwise, you will be folding the best hand too often.

Although you don't want to loosen up too much, when confronted with a late-position raise, it is frequently correct to reraise with hands such as A-T offsuit or 77. The reason for this is that your opponent may be holding an even weaker hand, such as K-T, A-x*, or 4-4. By reraising, you accomplish two things. First, you knock out

---

* Where we use x like this, it means any unspecified card.

the other players (unless they either have very good hands or are extremely stubborn), enabling you to play the probable best hand in position against one opponent. Second, a reraise allows you to take the lead in the pot. Frequently, the flop will be of no benefit to either of you, and your follow-up bet on the flop will convince your opponent to fold (partially due to the strength you represent by reraising before the flop).

Tip 9

It's okay to cold-call a raise with A-K.

This tip is not an absolute. There are situations in which a better play exists, and these are addressed here as well.

The problem with "going to war" with A-K is that it generally must improve to a pair or better to win the pot. There are times in which it is preferable to not commit a lot of chips before the flop; rather, you can *smooth call* (just call, that is, specifically not raise) a raise with your A-K and wait to see what develops. If you flop a pair, you can then kick into a more aggressive gear. By doing this, you tend to lose the minimum amount when you miss the flop. Also, you may win extra bets when you do hit your hand, as your lack of preflop aggression might cause your opponents to underrate your hand.

Basically, calling a preflop raise with A-K is preferable when you feel your hand needs improvement to win, and reraising is preferable when you feel you might be able to win the pot with just ace high. Let's see how you can determine which condition is the case:

Factors favoring calling with A-K:

- When you face an early-position raiser, this player likely has a good hand, probably a high pair or even A-K himself. Typical players do not raise with A-x or hands like K-J from early position. So, it is unlikely that your A-K is much of a favorite over most early-position raising hands. However, it improves often enough to justify a call.

- When one player has raised and a few players have called, you definitely have to improve to win the pot, since someone has either started with a pair or will make one. Also, should you flop a pair, it is possible that the original raiser will bet into the field, setting up an opportunity for you to trap the other players for a raise.

Factors favoring reraising with A-K:

- When the only player in the pot is a middle- to late-position raiser, you should almost always reraise with A-K. In this scenario, it is likely that the raiser has nothing more than high cards (or possibly a hand like A-x suited), and your A-K plays quite nicely against this type of hand heads up. So, your reraise has two objectives. You would like to get more money into the pot with the probable best hand. You would also like to eliminate the rest of the field, enabling you to play the hand heads up and in position. In this situation, you have two ways to win the pot: either with a bet on the flop, or by showing down your ace-high on the river.

- When the original raiser is a maniac*, you should probably reraise regardless of your position. The reasons for this are the same as those in the preceding point, since you would prefer to get rid of the other players, plus you will have the best hand most of the time.

---

* Maniac: Someone who bets and raises wildly and at every possible opportunity — with little correlation to the value of his cards.

Tip 10

Paying attention to your opponents allows you to more accurately read the strength of their hands.

Few intangibles affect your results in poker to the extent that your level of focus does. Simply by paying attention to the action, you can learn what to expect from each of your opponents. This does not refer strictly to the times you are involved in a hand; rather, you should be watching *every* hand, whether you are involved or not.

By focusing on the game, you learn which players play loose, tight, passive, and aggressive, and how their position influences which hands they enter pots with. Once you have a good read on their play, you can start developing effective strategies for beating them. Although adhering to a solid basic strategy will help you become a winning hold'em player, that alone is not enough. You must also make adjustments based on the other players in the pot. Poker is a *situational* game, and each situation requires independent analysis.

Here are two examples in which knowledge of your opponents allows you to make the proper decision:

Early Raise

You can't treat an early-position raise from a player who raises every fourth hand the same as you would treat an early position raise from a player who seems to raise only every fourth year.

This should be fairly obvious. The first player could easily have a hand like A-7 suited or K-J offsuit if he raises this frequently. Therefore, you should not be unduly apprehensive of this action. Instead, you should reraise with any hand that you would ordinarily raise with in your position. Ideally, the hand will then be played out between you and the maniac, and you should be holding the best hand most of the time.

But if it's the tight player who raises in early position, you must fold all but your very best hands. You should be saying to yourself, "This guy hasn't raised since the Carter administration. Just what can he have?"

The answer, of course, is only a few hands: A-A, K-K, Q-Q, or maybe A-K. So, it doesn't do you much good to call his raise with J-J. It's a nice hand in absolute terms, but this is the time to toss it into the *muck* (the discard pile). Also, if you are holding Q-Q, you are in trouble as well. Your opponent is *either* a big favorite with his overpair, or close to an even money shot with A-K. If ever there was a time to pass Q-Q, this is it. If you stick to playing only A-A, K-K, and A-K suited when a supertight player raises, you won't be contributing to his account.

Limp

Treat a limp from a tight player differently from that of a loose one.

When a tight player calls, he is far more likely to hold a quality hand than when a loose player limps. The tight player is not entering the pot with trash. Just because he didn't raise the pot, you cannot assume he isn't holding a quality hand. Tight-passive players commonly just call with hands such as T-T, A-Q, K-Q suited, or possibly even A-K and J-J. With that in mind, it takes a monster to raise the pot behind him. If you hold a hand such as A-Q or T-T, you are generally better off just calling a limp by a tight player.

Conversely, you can play aggressively behind a loose player's limp, in an attempt to isolate him in the pot. It is nearly always a desirable situation if you can play a pot heads up against a weaker hand. If a loose player has limped and you are on or next to the button, you can raise with any of the hands you would have played had it been folded around to you. This can include hands as weak as K-T, which still figure to have a decent chance at being the best hand in this situation. Plus, you hold the benefit of position.

Tip 11

J ♠

You are generally receiving good odds on your hand when faced with calling half a bet in the small blind.

♥

Suppose three players have called the initial bet. You are in the small blind with half a bet in. What price are you receiving from the pot on this call? You must put in half a bet, and the pot contains nine half-bets (including the big blind and your small blind) already. So, the pot is laying you a price of 9-to-1. This means you must win only 1 time in 10 for calling to be correct, assuming no additional betting. However, there *is* additional betting, and your positional disadvantage should also be considered here. Therefore, you should be holding a halfway decent hand to complete the bet.

A broad range of hands are worth a call, though. Any two suited cards will do, as well as any hand containing an ace. Also, any two connecting cards 9-8 or higher are worth a call. Hands with *one gap* (cards not adjacent in rank, but separated by one rank) smaller than Q-T should typically be folded (T-8, for example). Any pair is playable from the small blind. Some of these hands need to be hit pretty solidly by the flop for you to continue, but they do possess the potential to develop into big hands.

The preceding guidelines apply to games with a 1-2 chip blind structure (such as the $1 and $2 blinds in a $2-$4 game or $3 and $6 in a $6-$12 game), in which the small blind is exactly half the amount of the big blind. However, you may find yourself in a game with either a 1-3 or 2-3 structure. This has a huge effect on how the small blind should be played.

For 1-3 chip games, treat the small blind as you would a late position hand. If the hand isn't worth a full bet from late position, it isn't worth two-thirds of a bet from the small blind. Of the types of hands listed earlier as playable, suited trash and bad aces should now be folded, as should connectors such as 9-8 and T-9 offsuit. Small pairs are still worth a call, as are medium to large suited connectors.

In 2-3 chip games, playing the small blind is incredibly simple. If two or more players have called, you should call with everything! Yes, even 7-2 offsuit* is worth an extra chip in this spot. Just don't get carried away if you flop a deuce. The time to consider folding the small blind for one-third of a bet is when only one player has called, you are holding a bad hand, and the big blind is a frequent raiser. As long as those conditions aren't all there, though, you should put in the extra chip.

---

* This hand is singled out because it is the worst possible holding in any game with more than just a few players. In a short-handed game, 3-2 offsuit is the worst.

Q
♠

Tip 12

Call a raise from
an early-position
raiser only with
very good hands.

Q
♥

A raise from a typical player in early position nearly always signifies a hand of great strength. As a result, you must elevate your playing standards considerably. One of your goals in hold'em should be to try to enter pots with what you think is the best hand as often as possible. Calling early-position raises with a wide range of hands is not the way to accomplish this objective.

What hands are playable against an early-position raise? In the absence of other callers, if you stick to a very selective strategy of playing only A-Q suited, A-K, or a pair of jacks or better, you avoid putting your money in with the worst hand too often.

At first glance, it would seem that T-T is a good hold'em hand. And it is. However, when the first player in has raised the pot, you should ask yourself, "What range of hands is he likely to be holding in this situation?" If the raiser is a solid player, toss those two tens into the muck. The reason for this is that most solid players raise up front with only a few hands: A-A, K-K, Q-Q, J-J, T-T, A-K, and A-Q. Your two tens are a big underdog if your opponent has a pair, and only a slight favorite against A-K or A-Q. It is important to avoid these types of either-or situations in hold'em as much as possible, if you plan on winning at the game. Either you're a big underdog or you're a slight favorite.

However, if the early-position raiser is a loose or reckless player, you are playing too tightly if you fold your tens. The reason is that a maniac raises the pot with a huge number of hands that are *dominated** by your pair of tens, including smaller pairs, A-x, or even hands like 7-8 suited. Against this type of opponent, the correct play is to reraise in an attempt to play your pair heads up against the maniac.

---

* Dominated: The situation in hold'em of one hand being significantly ahead of the other, often because of having the same card in common plus a higher card. For example, K-Q offsuit is dominated by A-K offsuit. Also, any pair is dominated by any higher pair.

Tip 13

When a player in late position opens the pot for a raise, you should reraise liberally from the small blind if you plan on playing. ♥

There are several reasons why playing your hand this way is correct, all of which center around the basic truth that players open-raise from late position with less than-premium hands. After all, you do this yourself (see Tip 5).

What sorts of hands might you reraise with from the small blind? Against a raise from the button (unless he is a very tight player), you can reraise in the small blind with hands as weak as A-8 offsuit, any pair, or K-J offsuit.

For one thing, it is quite possible that you hold the best hand here. Your opponent on the button may have a hand like Q-T, A-3, or T-8 suited. It is never a bad thing to get more money into the pot when you have the best hand.

Also, by reraising, you will most likely cause your opponent to read you for more strength than you actually possess. This can come in handy later in the hand, enabling you to steal the pot on the flop or turn with a bet if the board is of no help to your opponent. What you have done is take the lead in the hand. Winning hold'em players play aggressively, helping themselves to the large number of pots that are there for the taking.

For another, the big blind will often call one raise, but not two. Generally, you would like to raise this player out if you have the opportunity, and send his blind money to the center of the pot. This creates a bit more value on your hand, with the presence of some *dead money** in the pot. You should particularly lean towards reraising a late position raise if the big blind is a good player, as you don't need him in your pot anyway.

One further benefit of reraising frequently from the small blind against a *steal position*** raiser is the psychological effect it has on your opponents. They will ultimately tire of your aggressive play, and think twice before raising when you are in the blinds. This may allow you to see more cheap flops than you should be entitled to, a nice perk generated by your aggressive play.

---

* Dead money: Previous bets abandoned in the pot such that the players who made those bets, having folded, cannot win the pot. Dead money includes folded blinds.

** Steal position: In a game with blinds, a late position, often the *cutoff* (position one to the right of the button) or button; so used because it is most likely from this position that a player attempts to steal the blinds, that is, open with a raise in the hope of not getting called by either blind.

Tip 14

It is a bad idea to raise very often from the big blind.

When you raise from the big blind, you are doing so for one reason only: to get more money into the pot. You won't eliminate players, as everyone who has called one bet will surely call another. Also, you will be out of position throughout the play of the hand, which negates some of your hand's merit, because you won't be able to *bet* as many decent hands *for value** from early position.

As a result, it is probably best to raise only with absolute premium hands from the big blind. Against several limpers, only A-A and K-K are true raising hands. While it is okay to raise with AK suited, you should be prepared to check and fold if you don't flop either a pair or a flush draw.

Against only one or two limpers, you can raise with a few additional hands, such as Q-Q, J-J, and A-K. The reason for this is that with only a few opponents, your big pair is more likely to hold up if one

---

* Bet for value: Bet a hand with the intention of getting called by one or more lesser hands, as opposed to getting the others to fold. This usually implies betting a hand that has only a slight edge, and one that a conservative player would likely check with. Also called *value bet.*

overcard* flops, and your raise gives you the lead in the pot. For example, suppose you have Q-Q in a three-way pot, and choose not to raise. Now, the flop is K-9-7. If you check, the next player is likely to bet regardless of whether he has a king, as he is attempting to win the pot based on the weakness indicated by your check. You are now in a position of uncertainty, which could have been avoided had you raised preflop and then bet on the flop.

The same goes for raising with A-K in a three-way pot. Had you just passed your big blind option and seen a flop of 2-7-8, your first inclination would likely be to check. By raising before the flop, though, you have built a pot worth taking a stab at with a bet. If your opponents don't flop a pair, they will be hard-pressed to call you.

Recommending not to raise with Q-Q from the big blind when several players have limped in may seem to contradict the advice given in Tip 13 about getting money into the pot with the best hand whenever possible, but this is not necessarily so. All you are doing is delaying the moment at which you choose to increase your involvement. With four or five limpers, it is fairly safe to assume that one opponent holds an ace, and another is likely to hold a king. Why not wait to see the flop before deciding if you wish to make a major commitment to this pot? After all, you are not in a position to protect your hand, as all the A-x and K-T hands are already in, and they will see the flop.

Now, if the flop brings overcards, you can check and try to determine if your hand is beaten based on the action behind you. However, if you catch a nice flop such as 2-4-T, you are in a position to take your opponents by surprise. You can either bet out or go for a check-raise, but either way you may win additional bets because your opponents have misjudged the strength of your hand due to your failure to raise preflop. So, you should be able to recoup those bets that would have been in the pot had you raised, and you can save money those times your pair is outdrawn by overcards on the flop. When you have an opportunity to play a hand in a manner that limits your losses but not your wins, you should capitalize on it.

---

* Overcard: A card on the board higher than the rank of your pair.

Tip 15

You can call more raises on the big blind than any other position, because you are halfway in.

To call a single raise, you always get a price of at least 3-to-1 on the big blind. The slimmest scenario is when everyone folds to the small blind, and he raises. More typically, however, you get a price of 7-to-1 or better to call. As a result, many more hands become playable.

When deciding if your big blind hand is worth defending, you must first pay attention to who raised the pot, and from what position. You should tend to play tighter when the raise is from an earlier position, or when a solid player has raised. You can be more liberal in your playing standards against loose or late-position raisers. For example, you should fold A-8 suited against an early-position raiser, but this hand is definitely worth a play when the raise is from late position.

Next, consider how many players are in the pot. The more players, the better your pot odds are. In multiway pots, some hands fare better than others. You should try to defend more with hands that have the potential to improve to better than one pair, since one pair frequently won't get the money when several players are vying for the pot. These include any pocket pair and medium to large suited connectors (7-8 or better). Simply having big cards in your hand doesn't justify a call in a multiway pot. The reason for this is that it is too easy to flop a pair and still lose, either to a bigger kicker or to two pair or a better hand. For example, suppose you call a raise in a five- way pot with K-J offsuit. (If suited, you *should* call.) Now, the flop comes J-9-6. If the preflop raiser had a legitimate hand, you may be beat already. Also, there are three other players to contend with here, one of whom may have A-J, 9-9, or 6-6. Another hand that may be out is Q-T, a hand that poses a serious threat to drawing out on your holding. All in all, a hand like K-J is highly likely to finish in second place in a multiway race, an expensive proposition in hold'em.

Contrast this to calling a raise with a pair of deuces. Although the flop is much more likely to bring improvement if you are holding K-J, the problem is that the improvement may either not be enough, or may help your opponents even more. With the deuces, though, you should have a pretty good idea of where you stand. If a deuce flops (which happens slightly more than 1 time in 9), you are in the driver's seat. This should be all the improvement you need to win the pot, regardless of how many players are in. As a result, you can play the hand very aggressively. Any player with top pair will likely call you down, and the more players in the hand, the more likely it is that someone will have flopped top pair.

Tip 16

You can occasionally reraise from the big blind against a late position "blind thief."

Although it is generally advisable to just call a raise on the big blind (since reraising is unlikely to eliminate any opponents, and just calling provides some deception about the strength of your hand), in some situations reraising is proper strategy. Remember, though, that the small and large blinds are different animals altogether. When you are in the small blind, one of the major reasons to reraise a late-position raiser is to knock out the big blind. Without this possibility, you want to reraise less frequently from the big blind than from the small.

Reraising from the big blind allows you to take control of the pot. As shown in Tip 13, the player with the lead after the flop often wins the pot when the flop is of no help to either player. Typically, whichever player gets the final bet in prior to the flop bets regardless of what comes, putting the burden on the other player to either call the bet or fold.

For example, suppose you hold K-Q offsuit in the big blind, and the button (a loose-aggressive player) raises. Obviously, you are at least going to call here, as the button could have a wide range of hands (most of which you can beat). Suppose you call and the flop comes 9-6-6. No help to you. It seems natural to just check and fold to your opponent's inevitable bet here, or perhaps call one time hoping to spike a king or a queen. However, what if you had reraised before the flop? This flop is unlikely to have helped your opponent either, and perhaps your reraise, coupled with a follow up bet on the flop, could have won you this pot. Your opponent could have Q-T just as easily as A-T. Either way, he is going to bet the flop if you just call preflop, but he would likely fold on the flop if you had reraised. So, your aggressive play has earned you the chips.

How low can you stoop in your reraising standards? This depends largely on the play of your opponent, as well as his position. For the most part, we recommend making this play (unless you have a monster hand) only against a loose player on or next to the button. This way, you are more likely to be up against an inferior hand. That said, you can make this play with hands as weak as A-8 offsuit, K-Q, or small pairs.

One final reason to reraise here is the intimidation factor. You are better off if the players in late position think twice before raising your blinds. It is sometimes helpful to make this reraise play once or twice early on in a session, as it helps set the tone for the session. If you are successful, your opponents will be more likely to wait for real premium hands before raising your blinds in the future, as they realize you are not afraid to challenge them. Poker is part psychological warfare, and making a few well-timed reraises on the big blind is an effective pre-emptive strike against the enemies to your right.

Playing on the Flop

Tip 17

If no one has bet yet, you should bet if you think you have the best hand.

This tip is consistent with the tight-aggressive strategy you should be practicing in hold'em. Because you are playing selectively, you have a good hand when you enter the pot. As a result, your hand tends to be better than those of your loose-playing opponents most of the time, even after the flop. So, you should play aggressively.

Bet When Checked To

In particular, this is true when the hand is checked to you on the flop. It is common for the flop not to have helped any player, and your bet might win you the pot right then. This is almost never a bad thing, unless your hand is so strong that nobody can catch up (for example, you flop four of a kind).

What exactly constitutes a hand worth betting on the flop? One of the main considerations is the number of opponents in the hand, as this has a major influence on how strong a hand is typically needed to win the pot. Several later tips cover this topic in more depth, but for now we establish some general guidelines for which hands are worth a bet most of the time.

Don't Be a Rock

It is incorrect to bet only when you are 99 percent certain you hold the best hand. Some players play hold'em this way, and they are commonly referred to as *rocks*. Don't be one of them! If you play like a rock, you won't lose your money as fast as someone who recklessly *rams and jams** every pot, but you will just as surely lose.

As a general rule, when the action has been checked to you (or if you are first to act), it is correct to bet anytime you hold the top pair on the board, or an overpair. So, if the board shows 3-7-Q, you should bet if your hand contains a queen, or if you have A-A or K-K. Also, bet any stronger hand such as two pair or three of a kind.

Betting a Draw

Betting a draw is also good strategy at times. The more *outs* (cards that make your hand into the winner) you have, the better it is to bet. For example, it is generally a good idea to bet if you hold K♡ J♡ and the flop is 4♡ T♡ Q♠. Here, you can win with any heart (flush card), 9, or ace. A king might win it for you as well. Added up, this draw gives you 18 outs (9 flush cards, 6 aces and nines that aren't hearts, plus three kings). With two cards left to come, you will complete your draw most of the time.

Playing a good draw aggressively is correct for two reasons. First, you might induce your opponents to fold, allowing you to win the pot without having to make your hand. Second, if they do call, you have managed to build a larger pot with a good draw, enabling you to win more if you hit your hand.

Lesser draws can still be played aggressively for profit, for the two reasons just stated. The possibility of your opponents' folding is enough justification for betting a straight or flush draw on the flop when it's checked to you.

Betting Middle Pair

Holding a hand like middle pair on the board is somewhat more

---

* Ram and jam: Bet and raise frequently and aggressively.

complex to play correctly. Generally, your position has a lot to do with how you should play this type of hand. Since you tend to be entering most pots with high cards, a good percentage of the times you flop middle pair occurs when you get a free or cheap look at the flop from one of the blind positions. Being in the blinds is a disadvantage to you, as you will have to act without much information about the strength of the hands behind you.

Thus it is usually best to check middle pair from the blinds if several players are yet to act. However, bet if only one or two opponents are in the pot with you, as you are likely to be holding the best hand. You don't want to give your opponents a free chance to catch up when you are in the lead.

In late position, bet your middle pair if it is checked around to you. You may very well be holding the best hand here. If several players call, you can see the turn card and then reevaluate your position in the hand. The same goes for virtually any pair when it is checked to you in late position. For example, you should bet if you hold A-3, the board is K-7-3, and everyone has checked to you. Most likely, everyone will fold if they are not holding a king. If you check, you are basically giving up the pot, as someone will probably make a better pair by the river. However, think twice before betting A-3 if the board shows K-Q-3, as it is too likely that some opponents will call you here due to the presence of the big straight draw.

Tip 18

When a player in front of you has already bet, raise if you think you have the best hand.

One of the inevitable side effects of playing hold'em is having to listen to your opponents whine about how unlucky they got in the last hand, the hand before that, and the hand last month when some < censored > caught two consecutive flush cards to outdraw their set. What you won't hear is how their demise could have been avoided with one simple action: a raise on the flop! So often it happens that a player calls a bet with a fairly strong hand on the flop, which in turn convinces other players to call as well. Had he raised, the player holding the best hand on the flop might have induced his opponents either to fold or make a very expensive call, both of which are positive results for the raiser.

Make It Tough on Opponents

When you hold the best hand, play it aggressively. Tip 17 encouraged you to *bet* whenever you feel you have the best hand, and this Tip encourages you to *raise* when the player to your right has bet, if you feel you have the best hand. Again, you need not be certain your hand is good to make raising correct.

You want to make it difficult for players behind you to remain in the pot. Raising serves to protect your hand; that is, it becomes very expensive for opponents to stay in the hand with you, and they will likely fold. This generally increases your chances of winning the pot, and that is a good thing.

Don't Give Them Odds to Call

Suppose you have K-Q and the flop comes K-9-5. You flopped top pair. If the player to your right bets and you are next (with a few players yet to act), you *must* raise here. Yes, it is possible you are behind. The bettor could have A-K or 9-9, for instance. However, most likely you have him beat at this point. The problem with just calling is the players behind you. If you call, they will probably call as well with hands like Q-J or A-9. Raising here relates to the concept of pot odds. You don't want to call and give your opponents a favorable price to overcall in an attempt to draw out on you. Rather, raise and take away the value of their hands. They may choose to call anyway, but you have done your part. They are throwing money away if they call — throwing it away to you. Don't give your opponents the proper pot odds to draw out on you.

Build a Pot

Another reason to raise a bet to your right when you feel you have the best hand is to build a bigger pot. There is nothing wrong with getting more chips to the center when you have the lead. Aggressive play will enable you to win the maximum with your good hands.

Don't Slow-Play

Some players choose just to call on the flop when they have a big hand such as a set or a straight. They want to wait for the "expensive" rounds to bet their hand. *Slow-playing** can cause problems, however. First, doing this will occasionally cost you the pot. By just calling, you may allow an opponent to see a cheap turn card that produces a *miracle*** straight, or helps him develop a good draw.

---

* Slow-play: Opting to not bet or raise with a good hand in the hope of trapping other players on this or subsequent rounds.

** Miracle: When poker players use this word, they generally mean the catching of a longshot, as, say, an inside straight or a third deuce when the player holds 2-2 against a higher pair.

Then, when you do later decide to put some chips into the pot, you may find to your dismay that you are the one who has been trapped.

A second reason not to slow-play is that players in lower-limit hold'em games typically call anyway. Why play deceptively when you don't have to? Slow-playing is generally done in an attempt to gain later action on a hand you feel you won't be able to get any action on if you play it aggressively right away. However, you rarely run into this problem in the games we're talking about, so go ahead and raise if someone bets.

Tip 19

When a player in front of you has bet, it's fine to call with a good draw or a medium-strength hand.

Although taking a raise-or-fold approach is typically the best way to play hold'em, in some scenarios it can be correct to call a bet from your right.

Good Draw

It is often best just to call when the flop produces a good draw at a complete hand. A typical example is when you hold a hand like 9-7 suited, and the flop is 3-6-T with two of your suit. You have 12 outs, of which nine make a flush and three produce a straight. (One of your needed eights also makes a flush, so you don't count it twice.) You are close to even money to complete this hand by the river.

So, should you be ramming and jamming with this big draw? Typically, you should not. One key reason for this is that your raise may eliminate other players. With this kind of drawing hand, you would prefer to have as many opponents as possible, since one of them may develop a hand that is second-best to yours, and contribute a lot of chips to your stack. You won't be able to raise out anyone holding a better flush draw anyway, as anyone with this hand would call your raise. The price you get from the pot will be better if you are up against several opponents, so don't raise with your draw if you feel it is likely to narrow the field.

Another factor to consider is that the original bettor has you beat at this point. Sure, you are likely to draw out on him, but you probably won't wind up with the best hand if you don't make your straight or flush. You do not want to raise and cut the field down to you and the best hand. Rather, leave the field in and give yourself a good price on your big draw. You'll win more money when you hit your hand, and lose less when you miss.

Medium-Strength Hand

Playing a medium-strength hand is somewhat trickier. With a hand such as middle pair, or top pair-weak kicker, you are often not sure whether you hold the best hand when the player to your right bets. Although making a raise might succeed in protecting your hand, you don't always want to commit a lot of chips at this point. Ideally, you would like more information about where your hand stands before getting too heavily involved.

If you are unsure of whether to call or raise with your hand, here is a good general rule to follow: Tend to call when it will be difficult for your opponents to outdraw you, and be more apt to raise (or fold) when your hand is vulnerable. Two examples illustrate this point.

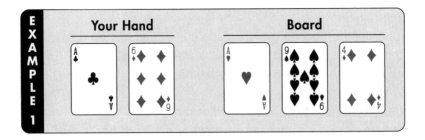

In Example 1, it will be more difficult for an opponent to outdraw you, so there is less danger in just calling a bet on the flop. If your ace is the best hand, it is likely to hold up with this board, whether there are two, three, or four players in the pot.

However, in Example 2, you are in a tough spot if the player to

your right bets, you are next, and a few players have yet to act behind you. This is a raise-or-fold situation for you. A call makes it easy for players behind you to stay in with hands like A-K or K-Q, which are drawing quite live against you. And, for one bet, they probably will call, but might fold when faced with calling a raise.

There is one additional benefit to raising with the two sevens here. Your raise screams out "I have a jack!," and this will probably cause a few hands to fold that have you beat — 8-8, 9-9, and T-T. Anytime you can raise and induce a better hand to fold, you have earned yourself a pot. Over time, the players who are capable of making these sorts of plays are the ones winning the money at hold'em.

However, you should exercise some discretion here. If you are familiar with the play of the bettor, and know that he is a very solid player, it is likely that you are trailing in this situation. You don't need to raise with your two sevens every time this situation arises. Against solid opposition, a fold is often the best play.

Tip 20

With a bet in front of you, fold if there isn't a good chance that you hold either the best hand or best draw.

Perhaps the biggest edge you have over your opponents in lower-limit hold'em games is your ability to fold. You often find yourself in games in which several players stay until the river, and then whoever winds up with the best hand wins the pot. If you make it a priority to remain in the hand after the flop only when you hold either the probable best hand or a good draw, you will be miles ahead of some of your opponents.

Some players believe in "taking one off" after the flop. That is, even though the flop didn't necessarily help their hand, they call the cheap bet on the flop hoping to develop some possibilities on the turn card. The problem with this strategy is that, with several players in the pot, the flop is very likely to have helped *somebody*. Often, they flop a hand that requires their chasing opponents to catch *runner-runner* (two consecutive improving cards) to beat them. Calling the flop bet in a six-way pot when the best hand you can make on the turn is a pair is nearly always a mistake, even if you hold A-K or A-Q. Your pair will often be someone else's two pair or flush card.

So, get out cheap and wait for a better opportunity.

When you hold a hand that stands a chance of winning unimproved — J-J for example — you don't need to catch another jack on the flop to stay in the pot. Flops such as 4-6-T are typically quite good for J-J, so play the hand aggressively. However, when overcards hit and several players are in the hand, it is time to get out. A good example of this is when the flop comes K-Q-6 or A-T-8. Against a large field of opponents, it's likely that someone has out-flopped you, leaving you with only two outs. You rarely play for two outs in hold'em.

Tip 21

In a two-way pot, play aggressively when the flop is A-9-3 rainbow.

In pots contested between you and only one other player, often the flop helps neither player. Therefore, whoever makes the first bet often wins the hand. Always be on the lookout for flops that contain few or no likely draws, as these boards are more likely to be of little interest to your opponent.

A typical such board is A-9-3 rainbow*. Since this flop has no straight or flush draws, and the presence of an ace means that there are no overcards to chase, it is extremely difficult for your opponent to stay in the hand without a pair. Furthermore, if his pair is smaller than aces he may give up if you bet, since an ace is a likely card for you to be holding.

So, it is imperative that you play these situations aggressively, particularly if your opponent only called before the flop. If he had raised, that would show a real interest in the hand, and you would probably have to show him the best hand to win. However, if he

---

* Rainbow: Of all different suits.

merely called preflop, then it is often correct to bet if you are first, regardless of what two cards you happen to be holding. The chances are great that he will fold. If you get called, no rule says that you must continue your bluff on the turn.

When your opponent is first to act and he checks, you must bet with this board. Again, it is very likely that your opponent is holding a hand like K-Q or 5-5. A-9-3 is a poor flop for these hands, and you should bet when he checks, even if you have nothing. There is free money in the center of the table, and you can make one small bet to lay claim to it.

On the other hand, what should you do when your opponent bets at this flop and you are next to act? It is good to have at least some knowledge of your opponent here, as some players bet only when they have an ace, whereas others bet lots of hands (perhaps themselves trying to pick up the pot). All things considered, here are some general guidelines for how to respond to a bet:

Your hand	Your action
middle pair	call
A-x	call
A-Q/A-K	raise
A-A, 9-9, 3-3	call — and bet or raise on the turn
A-9, A-3	call — and bet or raise on the turn

Tip 22

Guidelines on playing a flop of K-Q-3 rainbow

This advice applies to any situation in which the flop contains two face cards and one small card, without a flush draw.

Unlike the previous example, this flop is likely to have hit your opponent in some way, either by pairing him or by giving him a straight draw. As a result, you don't need to feel the same obligation to bet when it's checked to you as in the A-9-3 scenario. It is still okay to bet with a very marginal hand (A-T, for example), but you should have some outs to fall back on.

Against one opponent, it is correct to bet with a pair of queens or better, as well as T-J (open-end straight draw). If he is first to act and bets, call with Q-T or better. Also, raise with K-J or better. This is not a good board in which to slow-play a big hand such as Q-Q, since there are several straight draws present. You don't want to give an opponent the correct price (free) to draw with his J-9 or A-T, so make sure to bet your set here.

If there are several players in the pot, you need to increase both your betting and calling standards. Now, it is likely that someone is holding at least a king, so hands like Q-T have very little value when faced with calling a bet. Tend to fold this hand against several players. You should still be raising with K-J or better, however, partly due to the hand's value, and partly to give it some protection.

Tip 23

Guidelines on playing against one opponent when the flop contains a straight or flush draw

Anytime a straight or flush draw is present on the flop and you have only one opponent, you must be aware that a draw is a logical possible holding to be up against. If you bet and are called or raised, you can expect your opponent to be holding a pair or better, or a draw to a straight or flush.

In general, if you are first to act, you should bet when you hold second pair on the board or better. Also, bet with any flush draw or an open-ended straight draw, as these hands have nine and eight outs, respectively, to improve, in addition to the chance that your bet might induce your opponent to fold. It is good to take an aggressive approach when heads up if you have hit the flop decently at all, as there is value to be gained from your opponent folding. You don't want to give him a free opportunity to catch up.

If your opponent bets, you should call him with any pair, since it is possibly the best hand. Also, call with a draw to a flush or an open-end straight, as you have enough outs to justify staying in the hand for the small bet on the flop. When you hold any of these hands, you have at least a decent shot of winning the pot, and it is important that you don't give your opponent too much credit by folding too often here. You are playing too weakly if you do.

There are several hands with which you should be raising here. First, if you hold a flush draw and two overcards, you should raise. An example of this is if the flop is 3-5-9 with two hearts and your hand is K-J of hearts. In this case, you have as many as 15 cards that can win you the pot, providing a king or jack is good. Possessing this number of outs makes it more than 50 percent likely that you will improve by the river, making aggressive play desirable.

You should also raise with a straight draw and two overcards. If the straight draw is open-ended, as in the case of a board of 4-9-T when you have Q-J, you have eight cards for the nuts and six more that may make you the best hand. This is only slightly worse than the flush draw example above, and is still a situation in which raising is a good play.

If the flop is 4-9-T and you hold K-J, you have an inside straight draw plus two overcards, making 10 possible outs. Raising is questionable here, but can be the right play if you think it will stop your opponent from betting into you on the turn. Then, if you miss your hand, you may decide to check and see the river for free. This is commonly referred to as "buying a free card," and you can utilize a raise for this reason with any of the examples shown above.

One final hand to raise with on the flop is when you hold top pair, excellent kicker, or better. Now, you figure to have the best hand, and should be charging your opponent to outdraw you. Playing aggressively when you have the best hand is one of the surest ways to add to your poker profits.

Tip 24

Guidelines on playing against one opponent when a pair flops

Anytime that a pair hits the board, it reduces the possibility that the flop has hit your opponent's hand. The reason for this is simple. Having two cards of the same rank on the board takes away one of his opportunities to make a pair. Because the flop is less likely than normal to have been of aid, this is a good opportunity to play aggressively and seize control of the pot.

You Are First to Act

When you are first to act, you should bet if you have any pair (whether in your hand or from the board), as well as a big ace such as A-Q. Typically, these hands are the best hand at this point, but they are vulnerable, so don't give your opponent a free chance to catch up. It is important not to be afraid that the pair on the board hit your opponent's hand. Although you will occasionally run into trips (particularly when the pair is a high card such as A-A, which contains cards your opponent is more likely to play), you should not allow fear to sway you into checking.

In fact, if you sense that your opponent is likely to be in the pot with a weak hand — that is, something other than a pocket pair or big ace — it is correct to bet the flop when a pair hits regardless of your hand. The reason for this is that the flop is unlikely to have helped your opponent. In all likelihood, he will fold to a bet, fearing the possibility that you are the one holding three of a kind.

Opponent Is First

When your opponent is first to act and bets into you, call with any pair or big ace. There is just too good a chance that your opponent is trying to pick up this pot with a bet, and you do have a hand that can win without further improvement. If you fold a hand such as 8-8 when the board comes K-K-4 and your opponent bets into you, you are playing far too weakly. There is a very good chance your 8-8 is the best hand here. You won't win every time, but if you always fold in this situation, you are throwing a lot of winners into the muck.

If you hold an overpair to the board and your opponent bets, you should generally raise your hand *for value*. When you bet or raise "for value," this means you want your opponent to put more money into the pot because you probably hold the best hand. Your hand isn't a lock, but is most likely good.

You Flop Trips

Now, what should you do on those rare occasions when you are fortunate enough to flop trips? First of all, it's important not to get overly excited. Spilling your drink all over the table after the flop comes down is not a good way of encouraging your opponent to play along with you.

In general, you should tend to play your trips aggressively right from the flop onward. Most players expect their opponents to slow-play when they flop a big hand, so your bet may be interpreted as a sign of weakness rather than a showing of strength. This might lead to your getting unmerited action on the hand, particularly if you are up against a very aggressive player. By playing your trips *fast* (that is, aggressively, not slow-playing), you are taking advantage of your opponent's aggressive tendencies by turning them against him.

Conversely, you might need to check your trips on the flop against very tight opponents to suck any more bets from them. They are unlikely to call a bet on the flop, so you might check one time hoping the turn either makes them a pair, or induces a bluff. However, it is dangerous to give free cards when the turn can bring your opponent a miracle. So, it is best to check when fewer draws are present on the flop. For example, checking a hand like A-8 when the flop is 8-8-2 rainbow is fairly safe. It's probably not a good idea to check A-8 when the flop is 8-8-9 with a flush draw, however, as too many potential hands can either outdraw you on the turn, or at least develop quality draws.

Tip 25

Guidelines on playing when you flop a pair of aces in a multiway pot

For this example, we assume that four or more players are in the hand, and that the flop is A-9-3 of three suits. With no legitimate draws present, in all likelihood the best hand on the flop will win this pot.

If you are first to act, or if the action has been checked to you, you should bet if you hold an ace in your hand. You probably have the best hand, and you don't wish to give players holding hands like T-9 a free opportunity to *draw out* (improve against your better hand).

When there is a bet to you, you should raise with either A-K or A-Q. Only a few reasonable hands beat A-K or A-Q here (A-A, 9-9, 3-3, A-9, and A-3), so there is an excellent chance you hold the best hand. It is important to play aggressively, to maximize your profit from the hand. This is also a case in which many inferior hands (particularly any ace with a smaller kicker) will likely pay you off, so raising for value is a good strategy here.

What if you are the one holding the weak ace? We hope this means you are in the blind, not that you had a momentary breakdown in your starting hand standards. If there is a bet to you and your hand is, say, A-7, you hold enough to call but not enough to raise. One of the main arguments against calling (as opposed to raising) in general is that it gives your opponents the opportunity to draw out on you for free. However, given this board, your A-7 is highly likely to hold up *if it is in fact the best hand.* There are no overcards to an ace, nor are there flush and straight draws present. So, calling is not that dangerous here. By calling, you lose less money when you hold the worst hand, and probably win the same amount when your hand is good (since a raise on your part will tend to "shut down" an opponent holding a worse hand).

Sometimes there will be a bet and a raise before the action ever gets to you. In this situation, either one or both players hold a pair of aces or better, so you must proceed with extreme caution. There is very little chance that an ace with a poor kicker is the best hand here, and about the best you can hope for is to get out with a split. So, you should tend to fold in this spot unless you hold A-Q or better.

Tip 26

Guidelines on playing a multiway pot when two face cards flop

Again, we assume that four or more players are in the hand. For this example, the flop is K-Q-3 of three different suits.

If no one has bet yet, bet if you have a king or better, as this is probably the best hand. You can call a bet with a queen and a decent kicker. Your kicker should be a 10 or higher, as it is capable of developing a straight draw in addition to making two pair. However, if the bettor is a very tight player who bets only strong hands, it's probably safe to assume that your queen is not the best hand. Thus, it should be folded.

When facing a bet, raise with A-K or better virtually every time. Sometimes it is correct to raise with lesser hands, though, when doing so will help protect your hand. For example, in a five-way pot, if the first three players check, the fourth bets, and you are next with K-T, you should definitely raise. This makes it difficult for players with hands like A-J to call behind you. A-J poses some danger to your K-T here, as it can catch one of three aces or one of three tens. If a 10 comes, you are likely to lose several bets, as it makes you two pair. Players drawing with six outs are often correct to pay one small bet to draw. Your raise takes this play away from them, and makes it a mistake for them to continue with the hand.

If you hold J-T, for an open-ended straight draw, you should call. There is no point in raising with this hand, as all you will do is knock out the other players behind you. Since you are drawing to the nuts, and won't win the pot unless you make your hand, it doesn't really affect your chances of winning whether there are two or 20 players in the pot. It is good to keep everyone in, so that they can pay you off those times that you do make your hand. This is one situation in which checking and calling is the correct play most of the time. The main exception is when you think a bet might induce everyone else to fold, but in a multiway pot with two face cards on the board, someone almost certainly has a pair with which to *call you down**.

---

* Call someone down: Check, and call all bets to the river.

Tip 27

Guidelines on playing multiway pots when a flush or straight draw is present

The presence of some draws on the board somewhat complicates the reading of hands. When no legitimate draws are present, bets and raises signify made hands. With two to a straight or flush on the board, however, bets and raises occasionally are *come bets,* in which a player is pushing a drawing hand rather than a made one.

As in the examples given in the previous tips, you should bet if you hold top pair or an overpair to the board, both to help protect your hand and for value. If there is a bet to you, you should raise with top pair-top kicker or better. Just calling with top pair-lesser kicker is often best, unless a raise might narrow the field. You should have a good idea whether a raise will accomplish this objective based on your position relative to the bettor. If the bettor is to your immediate right, your raise forces all the other players in the pot to call double bets. However, if a player bets and several opponents have already called, all raising accomplishes is to build a bigger pot. You need a very strong hand to do this.

One hand you can raise with in this case is the nut flush draw. You have close to a 40 percent chance of completing your flush by the river, and if several players are "trapped" between the original bettor and you, you don't mind building a larger pot with a quality draw such as this. A side benefit of raising here is that the other players are likely to *check to the raiser* (you, in this case) on the turn. This way, if the turn card does not provide improvement, you can check as well. So, you save half a big bet those times the turn card doesn't help your hand, but you gain several small bets when it does.

For the most part, call with quality draws to flushes and open-ended straights. You won't win the pot unless you hit the draw, and you don't want to raise out any of your opponents. You gain nothing by narrowing the field down to you and the best hand. Your chances of winning the pot are virtually the same, but you won't win as much money when you do.

There is one notable exception to this, however. Sometimes it is good to raise with a drawing hand when simply making a pair might win the pot for you. Here is an example:

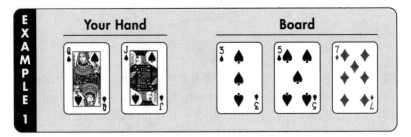

It is a five-way pot, and the first player bets. Although you won't raise out anyone holding a better flush draw, and your queen high is surely not the best hand right now, a raise might be the right play for another reason. Suppose your raise causes a player holding A-J or K-Q to fold. Now, you might win the pot not only if you make a flush, but also if you make a pair. In this case, you have created *extra outs* for yourself. However, don't take this idea overboard. It is best to make this play with two cards in the T-Q range, as they are most likely to be in *kicker trouble** should they pair up. That is, you want to drive anyone out of the pot who will have a higher kicker than yours if he pairs.

---

* Kicker trouble: The situation in which you have a pair, but if someone else has the same pair, he likely has a higher kicker.

Playing on the Turn

Tip 28

With most of the cards out, and the bet size doubled, you frequently fold on the turn.

In hold'em, you use five of seven cards to make the best possible poker hand. By the time you have seen the turn card, you know six of those seven cards, so you have a good idea of how the hand is shaping up. This is also the point at which the stakes double. As a result, the turn is not the time to chase, because you have only one card left, and it has become much more expensive to remain in the hand.

Therefore, you should fold on the turn unless one of the following three conditions is met:

- You are holding the probable best hand. If this is the case, you should usually raise if another player bets, or bet if no one has bet yet.

- You are drawing to the best hand. As always, you need to weigh the pot odds to determine if your continued involvement in the pot is justified. Generally, you are getting the right price to draw to a flush or open-ended straight. Also, if another player has obviously made a flush or straight, you can probably continue with a set (as you have 10 cards to improve). However, hands such as inside straight draws (four outs) or two pair when someone has a flush (four outs) should be folded, unless the pot offers appropriate odds to stay in the hand. In very large pots, you might call a bet with middle pair if you are convinced that hitting either the pair or your kicker will be enough of an improvement to win the pot. You have five outs in this case, and are at times getting enough of an overlay from the pot to make a call the correct play.

- You have been given a *free card* (that is, no one has bet on this round). Obviously, you are happy when everyone checks on the turn if you have a longshot draw such as an inside straight possibility or a pocket pair that needs to hit a set to win. Occasionally this free card allows you to win a large pot that you shouldn't be entitled to. The lesson here is that when you are on the flip side of things, don't give your opponents "free" chances to outdraw you.

Tip 29

Bet if you think you have the best hand.

Don't allow a player to catch a river card to beat you when he wouldn't have called had you bet the turn. If you are unsure whether you are holding the best hand, err on the side of aggression. It is much worse when a check turns a hand that would have been folded into a winner than it is to bet less than the best hand on the turn. The former costs you a pot; the latter costs you only a bet.

Your opponents commonly call the small flop bet with a wide assortment of hands, hoping for improvement on the turn. Then, they fold when confronted with the double-sized turn bet. You must follow through on your flop bet by firing again, as the turn bet packs considerably more punch. It is a cardinal sin of hold'em to lose pots by granting free cards to undeserving opponents. In fact, this may be the single biggest reason why some players who have good hand selection fail to win at the game.

Sometimes on the turn the best play is to try for a check-raise, rather than simply betting out. Ideally, the check-raise enables you to win additional bets when you hold the best hand. Make sure, however, that the following two conditions pertain when considering this option:

- You should be fairly certain your one or more opponents will bet when checked to. It is far better to bet and be called for one bet than to go for a check-raise, only to have the other players check behind you.

- If you check in a situation in which it might be checked around, your hand should be strong enough to withstand a free card. For example, checking the nut flush or a full house will generally not cost you the pot if everyone sees a free river card. However, if you hold 9-8 suited and the board is 2-2-4-8, anyone with overcards* is a major threat to draw out on you. So, it is best to bet this hand, because you cannot risk giving a free card to a hand like K-J or Q-T. These hands probably won't call a bet, but they are drawing very live — so don't give them a free chance to draw out on your vulnerable hand.

In addition to protecting your hand, it is important to gain value by betting the turn when you have the probable best hand. It should be your goal when playing hold'em to win every dollar possible. You won't do this by playing overly cautiously on the turn. Many of your weak-playing opponents will call you down with any pair or even ace high, so you will have a lot of opportunity to extract extra chips from them by betting when you feel you have the winner.

---

* Overcards: Cards higher than your pair, or cards higher than any on the board.

Tip 30

Usually raise when you hold the best hand and it is bet to you.

When you hold the best hand and someone else has bet, you are giving your opponents a free card if you merely call. There is little difference between checking the best hand if no one has yet bet, and calling with it once someone has wagered. So, once again, you must focus both on extracting the maximum from your opponents, and on how potentially catastrophic granting a free card might be.

As a general policy, you should raise a bettor whenever you hold a fragile hand that nevertheless figures to be the best at this point, especially if other players remain to act in the hand. For example, you hold J-J and the board is 4-6-9-T. Raise if someone bets and you are next, for two reasons.

- You don't want to give players holding overcards or other draws a cheap shot at the pot.

- You are very likely getting more money into the pot with the best hand, which is a good thing.

The time to just call a bet with the best hand is when you want other players to call behind you. This happens when your opponents are *drawing dead** or very close to it. Only a few big hands deserve to be played in this fashion — nut flushes, full houses, and four of a kind. And, you should *smooth call*** only when you feel this action will create a larger pot than a raise would, because you fear that your opponents will run for the hills when faced with calling a raise. If they are willing to call a raise on the turn, then by all means accommodate them.

---

* Drawing dead: Trying to make a hand that will lose if made. An example is drawing to a flush when an opponent already has a made full house

** Smooth call: Call, and specifically not raise, on your turn.

Tip 31

Usually check when you have a draw to the best hand and it has been checked to you.

This is a tricky one, which experience will help you navigate more profitably. It is tempting to bet the turn with only a draw when you are in last position, as nobody has shown much strength and you might win the pot with your *semibluff**. There are times when this is the correct play. Basically, if you are against only one or two opponents who you feel made weak calls on the flop, a turn bet is likely to win you the pot. If you are called, though, it is still possible that you will improve to the best hand.

However, most of the time you should check and accept the free card graciously. Simply because your opponents check doesn't mean they aren't prepared to call, and it is often to your advantage to get to the river as cheaply as possible when all you have is a draw.

One problem with betting the turn *on the come*** is that it can place

---

* Semibluff: A bet made on a hand that is probably not the best at the time of the bet, but that has two ways to win: either by getting everyone else to fold or, if called, that might improve on succeeding cards.

** Bet on the come: Make a bet on a drawing hand, that is, when holding four cards to a flush or straight.

you in a difficult position on the river. Suppose you bet a flush draw on the turn, hoping to win the pot, but are called in two spots. Now a *blank* * comes on the river. You are left holding, for example, the same Q-J you started with, a hand that probably has no chance to win in a showdown. The two players check to you again. What should you do?

Since you seized the initiative in this pot and cannot win by checking, you must bet again and hope that your opponents will release a small pair, ace high, or whatever they called with on the turn. Unfortunately, at this point the pot has grown quite large, and you are likely to receive a *curiosity call* ** from some sort of marginal hand. Many opponents will call hoping that all you have is a busted flush draw. In this case, they will be right. So, your decision to semibluff on the turn is actually a two-big-bet decision, as you must be willing to fire twice to try to win the pot. This is why it is usually best simply to check your draw on the turn and hope for the best, unless you have detected weakness in all opponents in the hand.

---

* Blank: Earlier we defined this as a card that doesn't help your hand. More generally, the term refers to a card that doesn't appear to help *anyone*. For example, if the board is K-Q-J-9 of mixed suits, a 2 on the river would be considered a blank.

** Curiosity call: A call from someone who is positive he is beat but just wants to know what you had, often accompanied by a statement such as, "I knew you had me beat, but I just had to see it," or, "I knew you had me beat, but the pot was too big to fold."

Tip 32

6 ♣

Generally call (rather than raise) when you are drawing to the best hand and there has been a bet to you.

9 ♣

As always, a major consideration in determining whether to stay with a draw is whether the necessary pot odds are present. You have to give up some of your lesser draws, particularly if the pot is small. Sometimes your draw presents a close decision between calling and folding. If this is the case, consider whether the pot can still be raised behind you. When the bet comes from your right, and several players have yet to act, you should tend to fold marginal hands, as you cannot be sure of how much it will end up costing you to stay in the pot. Conversely, if you are last to act (that is, the bet came from your left), it is correct to call more loosely, since you don't fear a raise.

Occasionally you can raise on the turn as a semibluff when you hold a good draw. However, as in betting a draw as discussed in Tip 31, this is often an expensive proposition. In fact, this play is riskier, as one of your opponents has already shown interest in the hand by betting. Raising with a draw on the turn is most likely to work when you have few opponents *and* when the bettor is a player you know to be capable of laying down a decent hand. Don't make this play against chronic *calling stations**; you will be handing them money if you do. For the most part, avoid raising as a bluff in low-limit hold'em games. Too many players will call you down, believing they are beat but nonetheless incapable of releasing their hands.

---

* Calling station: A player who calls on the least pretext, often with hands that rarely win against legitimate bets. A calling station is someone who feels he just has to "keep you honest."

96

Tip 33

Certain hands should typically be played aggressively on the turn.

Here are examples of hands that should typically be played aggressively on the turn:

- Top pair with a good kicker is likely to be the best hand. This is particularly true if nobody else has demonstrated much strength. Again, you should bet this hand for two reasons: to protect it, and for its value.

- Two pair, a set, or trips should be played very aggressively. Hands such as sets and two pair are often difficult for your opponents to detect, so they may raise you with hands like top pair or an over-pair. This allows you to win some big pots with your hand, provided you play it aggressively. Trips (composed of a pair on the board plus one in your hand) are typically an easier hand for your opponents to read, so you must play them with slightly more caution if you bet and get raised or reraised. If you raise when there is a pair on the board, and get reraised, you are likely to be up against a full house.

- A made straight or flush. The only real danger here (provided that the board isn't paired) is that you might run into a higher straight or bigger flush. For example, you might bet or raise with 7-8 when the board shows 9-T-J, but if you get reraised you must slow down. It is quite possible that you are up against K-Q. A similar situation involving a flush would be when you hold a queen-high flush and raise the bettor. Should he reraise you, you are reduced to calling him down. You should be willing to bet or raise once with any two-card straight or flush (that is, where you have both cards needed to make the hand in the hole; the situation is different with four to a straight or flush on the board), but to reraise it's best to be holding the nuts.

- You hold an overpair to the board. Most of the time this is the best hand, and you should play it as such. That said, if there is a lot of betting and raising, you may well be trailing. It is important to examine the texture of the board to help determine how strong your hand is. A few examples follow, with comments:

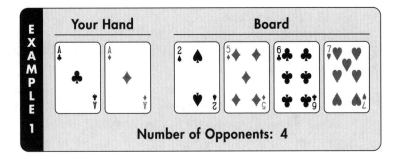

Comments on Example 1: You have the best hand if you are betting and they are calling. However, if there is a bet and a raise to you, you are probably up against either a made straight or a set. Fold, unless the raiser is a maniac who might make this play with any pair or draw.

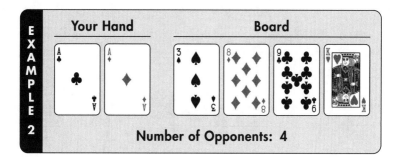

Comments on Example 2: Even with a bet and a raise to you, it is very possible that your two aces are still the best hand. The raiser might well be holding a king. The best play is probably to reraise, hoping to eliminate the other players. If you get called only, you are likely holding the best hand.

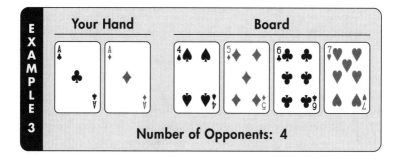

Comments on Example 3: Your hand isn't worth a dollar if there is any significant action. If a reputable player bets, you should fold your aces here.

Tip 34

What is a good draw to have on the turn?

Draw here means a hand that needs to improve to win. That is, although a hand such as two pair or a set can improve to make a full house, it is typically able to win the pot without further improvement.

The best draw is a hand that needs one card to make a flush and also is an open-ended straight, particularly if you might win the pot simply by making a pair. For example, if the board shows 2-3-T-J, two of which are diamonds, and you hold K◇ Q◇, a significant number of cards will make yours the best hand. You have nine flush outs, plus six additional straight cards. In addition, the six remaining kings and queens might make you a winner. This means that 21 of 44 unseen cards potentially help your hand, or nearly 50 percent of the remaining cards. Draws don't get any better than this, and it is correct to raise with this hand for value if there is a bet and a few callers. Of course, the more players who are in the pot, the less likely that simply making a pair of kings or queens will be enough to win. That loss of outs is offset by the increased payoff for making a straight or flush.

Other good quality draws include flush draws (nine outs), particularly to the nut flush, and open-ended straight draws (eight outs).

Note: Here is a word of caution about straight draws. If a flush is *already* possible, you might be drawing dead, or at the very least have lost two of your wins (as these cards put a four-card flush on the board). So, as a general rule, it is incorrect to draw to a straight when a flush is already possible. Also, the mere presence of a flush draw reduces the value of straight draws, as you are faced with the possibility that 25 percent of the cards that fill your straight might make someone else a flush. If two flush draws are on the board, only half your outs are totally "clean." This is often enough to make folding the correct play, unless the pot is very large.

Tip 35

You can avoid numerous dangerous situations on the turn in multiway pots.

This tip identifies and discusses common situations that can burn up your chips if you're not careful. We hope it will allow you to navigate better through some rough waters. These points pertain to multiway pots, those involving four or more players.

Playing Second Pair When Someone Bets
In a pot with several players, one of whom is betting, it usually takes more than second pair to get the money. So, throw this hand away. You have only five cards to improve (meaning only about one in nine times will the river card rescue you), and there are no guarantees that even making two pair or trips will be enough. Your two-pair card may make someone else a straight or a flush.

Staying in With Top Pair When Others Are Betting and Raising
Your play here depends upon a few factors: your knowledge of how the bettor and raiser play, the texture of the board, and your kicker.

- First, if the raiser is a very tight player, he can almost certainly beat top pair. If he has a set, you are drawing dead.

- Second, if there is significant action with a board containing a straight or flush possibility, it is likely one of those hands has been made. Top pair won't win in this case, either.

- Finally, if you don't trust the raiser to have a big hand, and the board is not all that threatening, you should examine the strength of your kicker. For example, suppose there has been a bet and a raise on the turn and the board is A-J-9-5. If your hand is A-6, you have an easy fold. However, A-K might be the best hand here. Against opponents capable of raising with any ace, you would be folding the best hand too often if you muck your A-K.

Staying in With Top Pair Against an Overcard on the Turn

When you hold top pair on the flop, an overcard comes on the turn, and someone else bets, most of the time this action is an indication that you just got outdrawn. Assuming this is the case, you are now left with second pair, analogous to the first example in this tip. It's no fun, but you should usually give up your hand in a multiway pot when this happens. You save money in the long run by doing so — and that's more fun than losing the money.

Drawing at a Straight when a Flush Is Already Possible

Suppose the board shows 4-5-T-J with three hearts. You hold K♣ Q♣. Not only do you have an open-ended straight draw, you have two overcards. However, life isn't exactly rosy. For one thing, you might be drawing dead already. If not, at least one of your several opponents surely has a heart in his hand. This means you might make either a straight or a pair, but still lose the pot if the card also puts a four-flush on the board. So, of your 14 potential outs (assuming you are even drawing live), only 10 of them are "clean," and it may be a stretch to think that simply making a pair will be enough.

Drawing at a Straight or Flush when the Board Is Paired and There Is a Lot of Action

Once again, we emphasize that drawing at one hand when a stronger one is possible can be a recipe for disaster. The more players in the hand, the more likely it is that someone might have a full house already. You won't be giving anything up if you choose not to draw at straights and flushes when the board is paired in a multiway pot. An additional consideration here is which pair is present on the board. If the paired card is one that people tend to play (aces, and to a slightly lesser extent, any face card), then it is more likely that someone has trips or better. Also, straight draws can be especially perilous here, as a player holding trips is likely to have another card in the same neighborhood. For example, if the board shows J-J-Q-3 and you have K-T, your straight card might make someone a full house. It is logical that you could be against Q-J, J-9, or A-J. Against the first, you are drawing dead; against the other two, you are drawing very slim, because in each case one of your straight cards makes a full house for your opponent.

Betting and Getting Raised by a Very Tight Player

If this happens, you are in a world of trouble if you don't hold the nuts. With some hands, you have enough to call. These include small straights, flushes, or two pair when the board doesn't show a straight or flush. About the only non-nut hand worth a reraise is a small or medium set, when the board doesn't contain *pat hand** possibilities. The reason for this is that the tight player may have A-A or K-K, hands you can beat with your set.

---

* Pat hand: Complete, or five-card, hand, that is, a straight or better.

Tip 36

You can get away from some decent hands in a heads-up pot.

Although you must not automatically give up hands like second pair in two-way pots, you may be able to bail out on the turn in some cases. If your opponent has bet the flop, and now bets again on the turn, this tends to indicate that he has a pretty good hand. Thus, it is generally correct to fold second pair at this point, particularly if the other player is tight. When playing against a maniac or very loose player, however, you just have to call him down and hope for the best.

Another situation in which you can probably save money by folding most of the time is when you have bet the flop with top pair or an overpair, only to see a "scary" card come on the turn and your opponent fires in a bet. Here are two examples:

Example 1

The board is 3-5-T and you bet the flop with your Q-T. A king comes on the turn, it makes three to a flush, and your opponent bets out. Although he might be semibluffing, it is very likely you are beat and drawing either slim or dead. So, fold and go on to the next hand, rather than spend two big bets trying to keep him honest.

Example 2

The board is 2-7-J and you bet the flop with your K-K. An ace comes on the turn and your opponent bets out. If he has an ace, you are down to two outs. And it is likely that he does, as that is the card most commonly played in hold'em. Also, your opponent isn't any more likely than you are to like that card if it didn't help him (thus less apt to be betting without an ace). It hurts to throw away kings, but you are nearly always correct in doing so in this case. Only against players who play with a good deal of deception and creativity is calling the best option.

Tip 37

What to do when faced with calling a bet with less than top pair is the toughest decision you'll have to make on the turn in a heads-up pot.

Although touched upon in the previous tip, this is an important and common enough situation to merit additional comments.

Here are three considerations to help guide your decision:

How Does Your Opponent Play?

You can call with a much weaker hand against an overly aggressive player. This type of player bluffs frequently, and it is often a mistake to fold any pair against him. He will just have to show you the best hand. Against a player who is ordinarily very tight or passive, however, it's a pretty safe bet that you are beaten, so you can confidently fold. In fact, you may even consider folding top pair with a marginal kicker against someone who is exceptionally tight.

What Is the Texture of the Board?

On a board such as 2-2-7-Q, it is highly unlikely that your opponent will bet both the flop and turn without at least a pair. There aren't any draws present, and your call on the flop alerted him that you have some kind of hand. However, if the board shows 4-5-9-T (and two of the cards are the same suit), it is quite possible that a hand like A-9 is good at this point. Your opponent might have a T or a 9 with a worse kicker, or be semibluffing with a straight or flush draw. You should be more inclined to call your opponent down with second pair when several logical draws are present on the board.

What Is the Pot Size?

Don't make the mistake of folding too quickly when the pot is large. A bad call costs you one or two bets, but a bad fold costs you all the bets in the pot, so it is far better to err on the side of calling if you are unsure about your hand. That said, the pot may have reached its present size because your opponent has been pushing a good hand, so you needn't always pay off with a marginal second pair type of hand simply because the pot has grown large.

Mistakes in Judgment

Don't be discouraged if you make some mistakes in judgment in these types of situations. It takes a great deal of experience to make consistently correct decisions, and even the best hold'em players make occasional mistakes. If you remember to consider your opponent, the board, and the size of the pot, you will have a good framework for making the right choice, though. On those times when you are still torn between calling and folding, however, remember that *calling with a loser is a small mistake, but folding a winner is a big one.*

Playing on the River

Tip 38

No more cards are coming, so all that matters is whether you have the best hand.

After the dealer puts the river card on the board, your hand is complete. At this point, you might have a big hand (such as a full house or flush), a decent hand (such as top pair or an overpair to the board), or a missed hand (such as a busted straight draw). If you feel you have the winner, you should usually bet when the action gets to you. If you are unsure whether your hand is best, you have the option of either checking and hoping for the best in a showdown or checking with the intention of calling someone else's bet.

Bluffs Rarely Succeed in Low-Limit Games

When you miss your hand, you might be tempted to take a stab at the pot by bluffing. A word of caution, however: Bluffing rarely succeeds in low-limit hold'em. With several bets in the pot, it costs you only one bet to attempt a bluff. This gives you a good price. (The pot might be laying you odds of 10-to-1 or better, meaning your bluff needs to succeed only a small percentage of the time to be a profitable play.) Nevertheless, in loose low-limit games, even 10-to-1 or better odds might not be enough to justify attempting a bluff, as someone will call you nearly every time.

A Good Bluffing Situation

One situation exists in which a bluff is more apt to be successful, however, and if you incorporate this play into your game it should increase your profits. Specifically, a good time to bluff is when you are against only one or two opponents, and a *scare card** comes on the river. For example, suppose you have been calling the whole way with a flush draw. The board shows: 5-6-J-7-8 . Now, any 4 or 9 makes a straight, and if you bet out with confidence when the 8 hits, your bluff has a reasonable chance of success. It won't work every time, but should succeed often enough to be a profitable play. It doesn't have to work even *most* of the time. It just has to work more than the pot odds indicate. For example, if the pot has five big bets and your bluff succeeds more than one-sixth of the time, you profit. Out of six times the situation comes up, say you lose one bet five times out of six, that's a loss of five bets. One time you win the pot, because your opponents fold, and that's a gain of five bets. That's exactly break-even. But if your bluff succeeds *more* than that (more than one time in six), you profit. Just don't make this bluff if one of your opponents is a calling station.

Another good example of a scare card is an ace on the river. Chances are, if your opponent is holding a pocket pair, he won't like the ace, and he just might lay down his hand. Of course, if he happens to have an ace, you will get called. That's why they call it gambling, though.

---

* Scare card: A scary-looking card for the situation. When two of one suit are on the board, the appearance of a third card of that suit may be a scare card for anyone for whom that card does not make a flush. If you had two pair when there were three spades on the board, you might worry about someone having the needed two spades with which to make the flush. And if the third of a suit is a scare card, the fourth suited card is even more so.

Tip 39

When to fold on the river if someone else has bet and you are last to act

Say an opponent has bet and you are the last player standing between him and the pot. It is now your job to determine the likelihood that you hold the best hand. To do this, you must consider not only your hand, but also the way the hand has played out. If your opponent has bet the hand all the way through, and there were no real draws out there, it is pretty likely that he can beat middle pair. On the other hand, if you were the bettor, and now your opponent bets the river when a flush card appears, you need to consider how likely it is that he has drawn out on you.

In this situation, you can put your hand's chances into four categories:

- **best hand:** you're 85 percent certain you have the winner
- **toss-up hand:** you have about a 50-50 chance of winning
- **longshot hand:** you have less than a 50 percent chance of holding the winner
- **busted draw:** you have virtually no chance of holding the winner

You should always at least call when you hold what you consider to be either the best hand or a toss-up hand. Since your chances of winning are 50 percent or better, you are getting the correct price from the pot to make the call. The more certain you are that you have the best hand, the more likely you should raise, particularly if there are some logical hands that your opponent might have with which to call.

The water gets murkier when you hold a longshot hand. Here, you need to know the size of the pot, so you can accurately assess the price you are getting. For example, if there is $72 in the pot and it costs you $8 to call, the pot is laying you a price of 9-to-1. Your hand needs to win only one time in 10 for calling to be correct. So, not only should you know how much is in the center, you should also be able to make a good estimation of your chances of winning the pot. With practice, you can develop this skill.

The lesson of longshot hands is that you can call fairly often on the river if you feel you have a decent chance of winning the pot. You need not be correct every time, or even most of the time, for calling to be the proper play. At the same time, make sure you are realistic. Don't throw money away in situations in which your opponent is 95 percent certain to have you beat. Experience and focus in the game help you become skilled at accurately determining your chances of winning the pot.

Tip 40

Bet the river with the best hand.

This might seem like an obvious statement, but it is amazing how often hold'em players check the winning hand on the end. They may think, "the pot is big enough," "I'd better check just in case someone caught that third four," or "I doubt anyone will call me, so I may as well check."

The problem with this is that the pot is *not* big enough, that four on the river is probably a safe card, and someone *will* call. It is very important that you do not *leave money on the table**. You must bet the river when you have the best hand, and collect those extra calls that your curious opponents will bestow upon you. This is one of the few times in poker in which you can bet and get a call from a player who has no chance to beat you. So, take advantage of the opportunity to bet the river *for value*.

When you are first to act, you should bet if you feel you hold the winner, because you are apt to get called by slightly worse hands.

---

* Leave money on the table: Fail to extract as much as possible (by not betting with what is almost certainly the best hand).

However, if you check, these hands might then check right behind you. The exception to their checking is those times that they outdraw you, in which case they would bet and you would probably call. So, those times you hold the winner, you cost yourself a bet or two by checking to your opponents. However, you still lose a bet those times you are beaten.

Tip 41

Usually raise on the river with the best hand if another player has bet.

To raise for value on the river, you must be fairly certain of a few things.

First, you should be confident that you hold the best hand. The problem with raising when you are only 50 percent sure that you have the winner is that some of those times you are wrong your opponent will reraise you. This will leave you muttering to yourself about what an idiotic raise you just made. A good guiding principle is not to raise on the river unless your chances of winning are 75 percent or greater.

Another important consideration is whether your opponent can call a raise. There are instances in which you feel your opponent is likely bluffing, but there is a small chance he has a monster hand. So, even though you might have the requisite 75 percent chance of holding the winner, raising is still a bad idea. This is because you cannot win an extra bet from your opponent. He will either fold if he was bluffing, or call or reraise if he has you beat. There need to be some logical hands that your opponent might bet and then call a raise with and still lose the pot for you to make a raise on the river.

Essentially, he must be capable of calling your raise with a worse hand for raising to be profitable. If it's an either-or situation, *either* he is bluffing and cannot call a raise *or* he has a hand that has you beat (no matter how unlikely that is), raising is not a good idea.

In a multiway pot, you may wish to decline an opportunity to raise for another reason. Suppose the first player bets, and you are next with a queen high flush. It is probably the best hand, and certainly one worth a raise. However, if several active players remain behind you, you might make more money if you just call. Your call might induce one or more other players to call as well, making you more money than had you raised. Furthermore, if the original bettor does happen to have you beat, your decision just to call doesn't provide him the opportunity to reraise you. Thus, you might win as much or more money with your hand by calling, and lose less if you do not hold the winner.

Tip 42

Bet with a toss-up hand if you are first to act.

There are several good reasons why betting is correct if you feel you have about a 50 percent chance of holding the best hand. Here are three.

1. There is a small chance that an opponent might fold the best hand. This won't happen very often, but you gain the pot when it does. You will never win a pot this way if you check.

2. You might bet a toss-up hand and get a call from a slightly worse hand. Had you checked, it is unlikely that your opponent would have bet his hand. However, he will probably call you. This is another situation in which you can win a bet on the river by wagering that you could not gain by checking.

3. Other times, your opponent has you edged in the hand. However, his hand isn't exactly a monster, and he may believe that he is in jeopardy if you bet. For this reason, he is unlikely to

raise, but will call. You lose one bet those times you bet the losing hand on the river. If you check, though, this same opponent would likely bet his hand. Since you have a toss-up hand, you call, costing you the same single bet that you would lose by betting the hand yourself. That is, it doesn't matter whether you check or bet in this situation, because you always lose exactly one bet.

Of the three possibilities, you gain by betting in two of them, and break even in the other. Overall, then, you are better off betting when first to act on the river if you estimate your chances of winning the pot at around 50 percent. You often bet losing hands by employing this strategy, but you also win extra bets and even the occasional extra pot that your more timid opponents do not. And, you can take comfort in knowing that many of those losing bets you make would often have become losing calls anyway had you opted to check. Thus, you're not really losing more bets than you would have by not betting your toss-up hands, and you're profiting by all the winning bets.

Tip 43

Check with a toss-up hand if you are last to act.

One of the contributing factors to the definition of a toss-up hand is that one or more of your opponents either had a made hand or were drawing to beat you. In the case of their having a made hand, it is likely that you are beaten.

When you are in last position and the action has been checked to you, it is incorrect to bet if you feel your chance of holding the best hand is only 50 percent. The reason for this is that of the hands you can beat, a good number of them will be unable to call if you bet. A busted straight or flush draw can't call, so you cannot win any additional bets from them. However, the 50 percent of the time you *are* beat, you can be quite certain that you will be called. So, there is little or no value in betting.

For a bet to be correct, or at least a break-even proposition, the likelihood that you will be called by hands you can beat compared to those that are better than yours must be about equal. This is not the case if you hold a toss-up hand, since a high percentage of the time the reason you win in those situations is that your opponents missed whatever hands they were drawing at. Don't bet the river *for value* in last position unless there is at least a 50 percent you will win the pot *if you are called.* If this is not the case, then check and hope for the best.

Tip 44

Call with a toss-up hand if someone else bets.

You shouldn't fold a toss-up hand on the river because, by definition, a toss-up hand is one that you feel has about a 50 percent chance of being good. Even if the pot is very small, you are getting the right price to call. In fact, there is really no situation in limit hold'em in which you should fold a toss-up hand on the river, as you should be getting a price of at least 3-to-1 or 4-to-1 on an even-money proposition. (This is called an *overlay*.)

One of the worst mistakes you can make in hold'em is to fold the best hand on the river. If you play long enough, you will occasionally be guilty of this error. Don't let it happen with your toss-up hands, though. With these hands, there is reasonable doubt, and whenever there is reasonable doubt, calling is far better than folding. If you start folding toss-up hands on the river in an attempt to protect your chips, you will have no chance of beating the game.

Tip 45

Playing a longshot hand on the river

Longshot hands are those you feel are highly unlikely to be the best on the river, based on both the value of your holding and the action in the hand. Typical longshot hands might include 9-9 when the board is K-Q-6-6-5, or Q-J when the board is A-J-T-9-6.

When you are in last position and it has been checked to you, you should check as well. Although you don't have a strong hand, you do have enough to show down. Thus, betting as a bluff is not a good option. Opponents who have your hand beat will call, and those who do not will fold. All that can happen is for you to lose a bet here. Just as in Tip 43, check, and hope that nobody has much.

If another player has bet, you have a far more difficult decision to make. You can't automatically call as you would with a toss-up hand, as you are beat here the vast majority of the time. Rather, you must determine whether the price you are receiving from the pot justifies your call. In a good number of cases, it is a close decision. If you never fold a winning hand here (that is, if you always call in these longshot situations), you are calling too often. The times you spend a bet "keeping them honest" will add up to more than what you win when your hand is good. However, by following the action and focusing on your opponents' playing styles, you should make the right decision most of the time.

Sometimes you reach what looks like a break-even situation; that is, the price the pot offers seems to match the amount you must invest to call. (For example, the pot offers 9-to-1 and you think you will win 10 percent of the time.) In these cases, consider an additional factor. When other players remain to act behind the bettor and you, lean towards folding your hand. The reason for this is that someone might overcall, and if that happens, it is almost certain that your longshot hand is no good. If you are the last player to act, you can call more often with your longshot hand if you feel the pot odds are close.

More
Hold'em Concepts
You Should Know

Thus far, we have presented concepts that deal with specific points during the play of a hand. We now present tips that are useful all the time.

Tip 46

Classifying your opponents helps you play more effectively against them.

Poker is a game of many different playing styles. This is one of the reasons why it is such a fascinating game. If you can learn how each of your opponents plays, you should be able to play with a greater degree of success against them.

How can you classify your opponents? In general, every player has tendencies that help define his play. A player can be primarily loose or primarily tight. Overlapping these styles, a player tends to play either aggressively or passively.

Loose

Loose players enter pots with a wide assortment of hands. They are the ones who cause you to ask yourself, "How could he play that hand?" There are different degrees of loose play to be aware of, as well. Some players play virtually every hand all the way with any possibility (however remote) of winning. Others play for one bet, but tend to tighten up if someone raises. Also, some players don't necessarily play many hands, but do defend their blinds to the death.

Tight

Tight players play very few hands. You won't see a tight player turning over too many marginal hands like K-9 suited, or K-J offsuit. Some players are so tight that the entire table takes notice when they finally do enter a pot. Obviously, when a tight player is in a hand with you, you must assume that he holds quality cards, and that a better than normal hand may be required to win the pot.

Aggressive

Aggressive players like to bet and raise, even if their cards don't seem to merit it. They are also more likely to bluff, so you must make more marginal calls against them. As we have seen, a loose-aggressive player is sometimes referred to as a *maniac,* and he is easily identified by his tendency to play a lot of hands very aggressively. Games with maniacs feature many large pots.

Passive

Passive players tend to call rather than bet or raise. *Loose-passive* players enter many pots, and call you down with weak holdings. These players have no chance in a hold'em game. *Tight-passive* players play only quality starting hands, but don't get full value from them due to their failure to bet when appropriate. You should be concerned when a passive player bets, as it usually signifies a very good hand.

The ideal playing style is *tight-aggressive.* You want to play tight, as you can't win if you enter too many pots. Rather, you should adopt a very selective starting hand strategy. But, when you do decide to play a hand, you should proceed aggressively. This way, you win the maximum with your high quality starting hand. Also, aggressive play has the added bonus of occasionally causing an opponent to fold a hand that is either the best at that point, or would have improved to win the pot. Passive players don't win at poker.

Tip 47

Paying attention while playing helps you learn to read hands better.

To apply this tip, it doesn't matter whether you are involved in the pot or not. You can really jump-start your game by closely following the play of hands when you are out of the pot. Not only will you develop a better handle on your opponents, but you will learn what sorts of hands tend to win in different situations.

What is the number one skill that allows the top poker players to be so successful? Is it their ability to sit patiently waiting for premium cards? Or is it their great success with timely bluffs? In reality, the top players are highly skilled in many areas, but what really sets them apart is their ability to *read hands**. In most cases, this skill was probably not a God-given gift. Rather, it is the product of much hard work as they progressed up to the top of the poker food chain. These top players have an ability to focus whether in or out of a hand on how the pot is played out. After enough trials, they develop a sense of what sort of hand each player is likely to have. Simply by actively paying attention

---

* Read a hand: Make a conclusion about another player's holdings based on that player's actions, remarks, betting patterns, etc., and on the constitution of the board with relation to the preceding.

in the game, you can learn to read the hands of your opponents.

Here is a checklist of what you should be observing about your opponents while out of a hand:

- **Level of aggression:** What sorts of hands do your opponents bet, raise, or reraise with? For example, some players have no problem raising with just a flush *draw*, whereas others only call even after they have *completed* the flush. Also, do your opponents bet after the flop with just ace high, or do they need a pair to fire in a wager? How often do they bluff? Do they play much more aggressively when they are in late position? Do they raise preflop with two suited cards, or do they need a pair or big ace to raise?

- **How position affects their starting requirements:** Some players play only top-notch hands from early position. Others disregard the importance of position altogether. Learn how the play of each of your opponents is influenced by their position by observing how often they enter pots from various positions, as well as seeing what sorts of hands they turn over.

- **Who bluffs, and who doesn't?** Learning this can help you save some bets on the river when a known non-bluffer bets. It also prevent you from making an ill-advised laydown against a chronic bluffer.

- **Who are the calling stations?** Observe which players refuse to be bluffed. Then, you can avoid trying to bet busted hands at them. However, you should be able to bet with a large number of marginal hands on the river for value against these players. Once you have identified a calling station, you can bet with hands as weak as second pair on the river, as you will be getting called by any pair or even ace high.

- **How liberally do your opponents defend their blind hands?** Some players automatically call a raise from the big blind position, reasoning that they are already halfway in. You can expect these players to show down a wide variety of hands. Others use more discretion, calling only with good hands.

This list can go on and on, as there are a number of things to look for. If you remember to watch the hand as it plays out, and recreate the betting after you see the hands turned up, you will begin to find patterns in the play of your opponents. Most hold'em players tend to play the same hands the same way time after time. Once you have identified some reliable tendencies or patterns, you can develop ways to exploit them for your benefit.

Tip 48

Detecting and using tells can add to your profits.

Just as you can learn about your opponents by observing how they play their hands, much can also be ascertained by watching their actions and body language. Many of your opponents tend to emit the same "signals" time and again, which you can use to deduce the strength of their hand. These signals are commonly called *tells* in poker terminology. Careful observation of your opponents can identify valuable tells, which will make or save you a significant amount of money over time.

Your many opponents exhibit a wide assortment of tells. There are, however, a few common ones to be on the lookout for. Once you are accustomed to spotting these tells, you will also become more adept at finding others. Some typical tells and their likely meanings follow.

Folding Out of Turn

If you look to your left before you act, you often notice some of your opponents preparing to fold their hands. They may not literally fold out of turn, but one glance at them alerts you that they are not going to play. This tell is helpful because it effectively alters your position. For example, one reason why you must pass some decent hands from middle position is that you don't know yet what your opponents behind you are going to do. However, if it is obvious that they are going to fold, you have just "inherited" the button. So, you can now play hands appropriate to that position.

Placing Chips on Their Cards

When an opponent places a chip on his cards, it usually means that he is going to play his hand. If you look to your left and observe this, it may help you avoid getting involved with a weaker hand. Be careful interpreting this tell, however. Some players always place a chip on their cards before the action has reached them. Your job is to ascertain which players do this only when they are going to play.

Picking Up Chips Out of Turn

Some players like to have their chips ready for action when it's their turn. They count out the amount of the bet, or even the size of a raise. Again, by looking to your left, you may be able to accurately predict what each of your opponents is going to do. This can help you avoid making marginal calls, especially if you see that the pot is going to be raised behind you. Be aware of the reverse of this tell. Some players habitually pick up chips when they intend to fold for any bet, perhaps in an attempt to discourage those bets.

Talking About Their Hands

Some players like to talk about their hands, or offer friendly advice to their opponents in the midst of a pot. What you want to know is, do they speak the truth? Should you believe them? In most cases, talkers follow a consistent pattern. Some players consistently lie, while others tell the truth in an attempt at reverse psychology. Learning to discern who falls into which category will make you some money.

Academy Award Performances

There is a good reason why most poker players don't get major roles in Hollywood. If you don't know what that is, watch them as they try to convince you to call, fold, raise, or whatever it is that they want you to do. Some players act strong when they are weak, reaching for their chips as they see you preparing to bet. Others appear disinterested in the pot until the action gets to them, at which time they ease in a half-hearted raise (while holding the nuts). By observing the table when you are not involved in a hand, you learn to identify the actors. Then, when you do play a pot with them, you are able to decipher their acts.

When to Look for Tells

The best time to learn to identify and use tells is not when you are actually involved in a hand. Rather, this is one more part of your poker education that can be enhanced when you have folded and are waiting for the next hand to start. The vast majority of your opponents use this time to chat, watch television, or schmooze with the cocktail waitresses. If you use this time wisely, you will be miles ahead of the other players, even if it costs you a date or two with a waitress.

Tip 49

When to bluff in limit hold'em

Although it may appear that successfully bluffing in low limit hold'em is a next-to-impossible endeavor, you can take advantage of some opportunities. Here are some dos and don'ts to guide you as you prepare to steal:

Dos

Do bluff against two opponents or fewer. Often in situations against only one or two players, neither of your opponents has much of a hand. Often both have been on draws that never materialized. As your hand-reading skills develop, you will learn when bluffs have the greatest chance of success, and you can limit your attempts to those times.

Do bluff when scare cards hit. We discussed this in Tip 38, but it is worth repeating. A bluff has a much better chance of success if your opponents can fold confidently. Bluffing when a random card comes often leads to calls out of curiosity as much as any other reason. However, when the fourth card of a suit appears, or the fourth consecutive card to a straight, or possibly when the board double-pairs, it should seem pretty obvious what you hold if you bet. Now, your opponents can fold, convinced not only *that* they are beat, but also of *how* it happened.

Do bluff when an aggressive player shows weakness. Aggressive players tend to bet when they have anything at all (and sometimes when they don't). So, if they check, it often means that they have given up on the hand. Although they may be checking something like middle pair (which they will call you with), it is probably worth a shot to bluff in this spot, as you know they can't have too much.

Don'ts

Don't attempt to steal multiway pots. Someone nearly always calls a bet when five or more players are in the hand. Your opponents often realize that a stronger hand is required to win in this situation; consequently, they may choose to check and call with all but their best hands.

Don't bluff behind a passive player's check. Passive players check hands that aggressive players routinely bet for value. So, don't make the mistake of interpreting a passive player's check as a sign of weakness. Rather, it's just an indication that he does not hold the nuts. It certainly doesn't mean you won't get called, though, so save your bluff for a better time.

Don't bluff when chronic calling stations are in the pot. These players often call with next to nothing. If you are the one holding *nothing*, then a calling station's hand will win. You are throwing away money if you try to bluff these guys.

Tip 50

Going on tilt will destroy your bankroll.

This tip is here for encouragement, although the wording may not appear to be uplifting. *Tilt* is a poker player's enemy when it happens to him, and friend when it happens to other players in the game. You can use tilt to your advantage by not falling victim to it, even though your opponents do.

What is tilt? Quite simply, tilt occurs when a run of bad luck causes a player to make irrational decisions in a poker game, letting emotion guide him instead of reason. Tilt can be instigated by the turn of a single unfortunate card, or as the culmination of a two-week streak of bad luck. Each player has a different "tilting point," and it is important to recognize your own.

Unfortunately, it is often extremely difficult to admit to yourself when enough is enough. If you insist on staying in a game after you have reached your tilting point, you are likely to "tilt off" a significant number of chips to your undeserving opponents. Any player who is able to admit to himself when he is emotionally unfit to play further, perhaps due to some bad luck in the game, and is strong enough to stand up and leave, is way ahead of the competition.

A true understanding of the nature of poker is one of the best ways to avoid going on tilt. You should realize that this game has an incredible amount of short-term luck, allowing less skilled or even poor players to win improbably for extended periods of time. Don't be discouraged by this, though; rather, realize that this is the lure for the weaker players. If the best players always won, there wouldn't be any poker games. The losers would take up War or some other game in which they had a fighting chance.

Every poker player at one time or another endures a seemingly endless bad streak in which his A-A or K-K never seems to hold up, his A-K is consistently greeted with a flop of 7-8-9, and his J-J is pummeled by a flop of A-K-5. What you must realize when this is happening to you is that you are not alone. This is simply part of the inevitable statistical deviations in the game. It will happen to you just as surely as it happens to everyone else at one time or another. By the way, it is generally not recommended to share your pain with your neighbors in a poker game. Although they may pretend to lend a sympathetic ear, they aren't really listening. They are simply waiting for a pause into which they might insert their own tales of woe.*

You must remember that poker is a long-run proposition. It is of key importance that you play correctly in all situations, even on days when nothing is going right. If you give in and start "playing like them," you will just lose more money. Regardless of how well you play, though, you will have some losing days. It should be your goal to walk away from these losing sessions saying to yourself, "I lost $100 today, but any other player would have lost $300."

Striving for perfect play, rather than perfect results, should ultimately help you to avoid going on tilt. If you can come to terms with the fact that occasionally someone will hit a 40-to-1 draw on you, you will be better equipped to handle the swings of the game. Focus on what you can control, and you will maintain the emotional balance necessary to beat the game. And, if you feel that balance slipping away, quit the game for the day, week, or month — until you have regained your composure.

---

* These are called *bad-beat stories*. No one wants to hear yours, and you won't want to hear those of others.

Tip 51

Practicing good game selection adds to your profits.

Recognizing profitable games is an underrated poker skill. It is quite possible that a player adept at choosing the right game wins significantly more money than a far more skilled player who lacks judgment in game selection. Do not underestimate the value of choosing the right game. Here are some guidelines:

- **Don't sit in games full of tight-aggressive players.** This is the style of play that gets the money in hold'em. If several of these players are in your game, they snatch up whatever profit is available from the weaker players. Look for another game.

- **Look for games with loose-passive players; those are the easiest games to beat.** This implies that the most profitable games may not have the biggest pots, as passive play tends to promote smaller pot sizes. However, these players won't charge you the maximum when they hold the best hand. Provided you don't return the favor, the chips will be heading in your direction.

- **Avoid wild and crazy games when your bankroll is short.** Games with big pots are appealing, but may not be your best move when you are on short money. You will have both your biggest wins and biggest losses in wild games. It is often best to seek out more passive opposition, particularly when you cannot afford a big loss.

- **Winning at poker is all about the edge you have over your opponents.** Poker is a long-term proposition, and if you play in situations in which you have an advantage, you will be a long term winner. You must objectively seek out games in which you do have an edge, and avoid games in which you do not.

- **That said, it may still be correct occasionally to sit in a game that you can't beat, due to the presence of a few excellent players in the game.** You are doing this for educational purposes, as you will spend your time in this game observing everything the experts do, so that you can replicate it in your own play. Just don't do this at a limit you cannot afford.

- **It's okay to play with great players, as long as bad ones are present.** In limit hold'em, the amount of money you lose to players who are better than you is much smaller than the amount you win from very poor players. This is true, of course, only if you are at least a fairly good player. So, don't be afraid to sit in a game with a few players whom you identify as being extremely skillful, if some poor players are there as well. Most of your profit will come from these bad players. Also, the experts will likely stay out of your way most of the time, allowing you to play mainly against the live ones*. You are much better off in this type of game than in one in which every player is fairly good, although none is exceptional.

---

* Live one: A very loose player, usually implying one who loses.

Tip 52

When to move up

If you have experienced success (or at least gained experience) at hold'em at one limit, you will probably consider playing in a bigger game at some point. This is particularly true if you have been successful, as the possibility of winning significantly more money at a higher limit is a strong incentive to step up.

Before you do so, however, you must make sure you are adequately bankrolled for the move. This is not a concern if your bankroll is renewable, but if you fear going broke, you should adhere to certain guidelines. In general, assuming you are a winning player, many experts recommend a bankroll of approximately 300 big bets to remove the risk of going broke.

The better you play compared to your opponents and the smaller the game, the less strict that figure need be. In general, though, for a $2-$4 hold'em game, you should have a bankroll between $600 and $1000 to "weather the storms." Someone with equivalent skills ought to have a bankroll of $12,000 for a $20-$40 game. And for a $50-$100 game, $30,000 to $50,000. And "bankroll" here means money set aside specifically for poker. It does not include the "rent money" or your savings.

Simply *having* the bankroll to move up does not mean that it is necessarily in your best financial interest to do so. It is probably best not to increase limits until you have become a consistent winner at your current level. One incentive you might choose to provide for yourself is to force yourself to *win* at your current level the required bankroll for the next highest limit. When you have increased your bankroll to the necessary level, you can step up.

Limit Versus No-Limit

There are some basic differences between what is correct in limit and no-limit play.

Although the mechanics of limit and no-limit hold'em are the same — in that players receive two cards and use them in conjunction with the five board cards — that is where the similarities stop. Some players are proficient at both forms of poker, but it is a mistake to assume that being a good limit hold'em player automatically makes you effective at no-limit. Here, then, are a few fundamental differences in the two variations:

- It is rarely, if ever, correct to limp in if no one has yet entered a pot in limit hold'em. However, opening a pot by calling is a viable no-limit play employed by many of the top no-limit players. There are a few reasons for this.

  First, it is absolutely essential for a good no-limit player to mix up his play. An occasional limp when first in helps keep your opponents off guard, particularly if you limp with a variety of hands (sometimes two aces, sometimes 7-8 suited).

  Second, in limit hold'em, if you limp in and are raised, the strongest action you can take when it gets back to you is to reraise one more unit, a play that will succeed only in building a bigger pot that you must then play against the raiser while out of position (unless the raise came from one of the blinds). However, in no-limit hold'em, you can limp in, get raised, and then have the option of reraising as much as you like. This grants your hand considerably more leverage, as well as providing you with an opportunity to really trap your opponents when you are holding a monster hand such as aces or kings.

Another incentive to limp is that no-limit hold'em is a game of implied odds*. As a result, there are many instances in which it is correct to try to see a flop cheaply with a weaker hand that has the potential to develop into a big hand. An example would be a small pocket pair or a suited ace with a small kicker. These types of hands can capture a big pot if they connect with the flop, but the amount these hands can win in limit hold'em is somewhat limited by the betting structure.

- How draws are played is much different in no-limit versus limit hold'em. Suppose four people have called before the flop, and you call on the button with A-T of spades. Now, the flop comes 6-8-Q with two spades. In limit hold'em, if everybody checks to you, you can definitely bet this hand. You might make your flush, catch an ace, or have everyone fold.

However, in no-limit, it is far more dangerous to make a bet with this draw. The reason for this is that one of your opponents may make a large check-raise, forcing you either to fold your nut flush draw or make a marginal, oftentimes bad, call. If you have a short stack, it is fine to bet some or all of your chips with your draw, as you don't mind being committed to this hand. You will either win the pot uncontested, get called and make your hand, or get called and miss. Thus, there is considerable value in betting. However, if you have lots of chips, but only make a fairly small bet on the flop, folding is likely to be the correct play if you get check-raised. For this reason, it is usually best to take the free card when your stack is deep, but to bet the draw aggressively when short-stacked. One point to add is that when you are on a short stack, the chips in the middle mean more to your stack than if you have a big stack, so there is more incentive to try to win them right away.

---

* Implied odds: The ratio of what you should win (including money likely to be bet in subsequent rounds) on a particular hand to what the current bet costs.

- You can protect your hand more effectively in no-limit. Since you can make any size bet you want in no-limit, your good hands are less likely to be outdrawn than in limit. This is because you will be able to make large bets that make it difficult for your opponents to remain in the pot.

- Early in no-limit tournaments, huge implied odds situations exist. No-limit is a game of implied odds. Top no-limit players don't mind seeing a cheap flop with an inferior starting hand, in an attempt to catch a lucky flop and double up. The key here is to recognize when your hand has improved enough to merit "going to war." There is a good reason why some hands are inferior — they wind up making the runner-up hand quite often. However, as your hand-reading skills evolve, you too will be able to see some extra flops hoping to "get lucky." Typical hands that have good implied odds are small pairs (should you flop a set against an overpair, you will get paid off handsomely), or suited aces (with which you can make either aces up against a hand like A-K or A-Q, or, preferably, a flush). The key here is that a small initial investment can yield a big reward. Although these types of hands can also win some nice pots in limit hold'em, they hold nowhere near the same value as in no-limit.

Appendix

To succeed at hold'em, you should have a good working knowledge of odds and probability. Whether you do the computations in your head on the spot, or take some time to learn by rote the odds of making certain draws, you should not neglect this aspect of the game. The chart on page 149 contains the odds for completing various draws in hold'em.

Notes on the Odds Chart:

- **# of Outs** — Total number of cards in the deck that will improve your hand enough to (probably) win.

- **Sample Situation** — The most common drawing situations for a given number of outs. This is not a comprehensive list; there are other potential draws.

- **After the Flop (2 cards to come)** — The chances of hitting one of your out cards either on the turn or the river, with only three cards on the board.

- **After the Turn (1 card to come)** — The chances of hitting one of your out cards on the river, with four cards already on the board.

- "Straight draw" means either an open-ended or double-gut-shot straight draw. (Both situations will complete a straight with two different cards.)

- "Flush draw" means that you already have four cards of the same suit, and need only one more. Completing a runner-runner flush draw (you have three flush cards and need two more) is much less likely.

- "Live overcards" means that you have one or two cards higher than anything on the board and you think making one of those higher pairs will be enough to win.

- If you'd like to calculate the chances of specific hand combinations among multiple players, there is a poker odds calculator available online at **www.CardPlayer.com**.

Post-Flop Drawing Chances (Approximate)

# of Outs	Sample Situation	After the Flop (2 cards to come)	After the Turn (1 card to come)
21	straight draw, flush draw, with two live overcards	70%	45%
20		68%	44%
19		65%	41%
18	straight draw, flush draw, with one live overcard	62%	39%
17		60%	37%
16		57%	35%
15	straight draw with a flush draw	54%	33%
14		51%	30%
13	flush draw with an inside (or gut-shot) straight draw	48%	28%
12	flush draw with one live overcard	45%	26%
11	straight draw with one live overcard	42%	24%
10		38%	22%
9	flush draw	35%	20%
8	straight draw	32%	17%
7		28%	15%
6	you have two live overcards, and need to make a pair	24%	13%
5	you have one pair, but need to hit your kicker for two pair or make three of a kind	20%	11%
4	inside (gut-shot) straight draw; also, you have two pair but need to make a full house	17%	9%
3	you have one pair, but need to hit your kicker for two pair	13%	7%
2	you have a pocket pair, but need to make a set (three of a kind)	8%	4%
1	you have three of a kind, but need to make four of a kind	4%	2%
7/10	you have three of a kind, but need to make a full house*	36%	22%

---

* The chances of making a full house (starting with three of a kind) are listed separately at the bottom because there are 7 outs on the flop, and 10 outs on the turn.

Glossary

active player: A player still in contention for a pot.

aggressive: Pertaining to a style of play characterized by much betting, raising, and reraising. This is not the same as *loose* play. Some of the best players are very selective about the cards they play, but when they do get into a pot, play those cards aggressively.

all in: Out of chips, due to having put one's remaining chips into the current pot, while other active players still have more chips and have the option of further betting.

ante: One or more chips put into each pot by each player before the cards are dealt. An ante is not part of a player's next bet, as opposed to a *blind*, which usually is.

bad beat: The situation in which a strong hand is beaten by a longshot or improbable hand.

bad beat story: A story told by someone who lost a pot, often a big one, in a *bad beat*. Usually no one but the teller is interested in hearing the story.

bet for value: Bet a hand with the intention of getting called by one or more lesser hands, as opposed to getting the others to fold. This usually implies betting a hand that has only a slight edge, and one that a conservative player would likely check with. Also called *value bet*.

bet on the come: Make a bet on a drawing hand, that is, when holding four cards to a flush or straight.

big blind: The player two positions to the left of the button puts chips into the pot equal to size of the limit of the game. Those chips (and the player who puts the chips in) are called the *big blind*.

blank: A card, usually turn or river, that doesn't help your hand. This term also refers to a card that doesn't appear to help *anyone*. For example, if the board is K-Q-J-9 of mixed suits, a 2 on the river would be considered a blank.

blind: A bet put in by a player before he gets his cards. A *blind* is part of that player's bet if he comes into the pot, as opposed to an *ante*, which just "belongs to the pot." See also *small blind* and *big blind*.

blind thief: Someone who steals the blind, that is, opens a pot without having good cards, hoping the blinds will just throw their cards away and the opener can win the chips represented by the blind or blinds without having to actually play the hand.

button: The disk or other marker that indicates the dealer position in a game dealt by a house dealer. Also known as *dealer button*.

call someone down: Check, and call all bets to the river.

calling station: A player who calls on the least pretext, often with hands that rarely win against legitimate bets. A calling station is someone who feels he just has to "keep you honest."

cap: The maximum number of raises in a round of betting.

chances: The likelihood of a particular event, usually expressed in the form of some kind of fraction or in the form of one number *out of* or *in* another. Compare with *odds*, in which the outcome is expressed as one number *to* another number.

chase: Try to catch a better hand with a worse holding.

check: Make no bet, but still hold your cards. You can check, and then call a later bet, fold when the action gets back to you, or raise.

check-raise: Check, often with a good hand, and then, when someone bets and it returns to you, raise.

community cards: The upcards dealt to the center of the table that are part of each player's hand.

complete hand: Five cards that constitute a straight or better. Also called *pat hand.*

counterfeited: Having a probable winner turned into a probable loser by the appearance on the board of another card of the same rank or suit as one of yours.

curiosity call: A call from someone who is positive he is beat but just wants to know what you had, often accompanied by a statement such as, "I knew you had me beat, but I just had to see it," or, "I knew you had me beat, but the pot was too big to fold."

dead money: Previous bets abandoned in the pot such that the players who made those bets, having folded, cannot win the pot. Dead money includes folded blinds.

dealer button: See *button.*

discards: The players' thrown-away cards, sometimes together with the undealt cards that remain in the deck. Sometimes called *muck.*

dominated: The situation in hold'em of one hand being significantly ahead of the other, often because of having the same card in common plus a higher card. For example, K-Q offsuit is dominated by A-K offsuit. Also, any pair is dominated by any higher pair.

double gut-shut: A five-card combination with two "holes," such that any of eight cards can make it into a straight.

downcard: An unexposed part of a player's hand, delivered face down by the dealer.

draw: An unmade hand.

drawing dead: Trying to make a hand that will lose if made. An example is drawing to a flush when an opponent already has a made full house

drawing hand: Four cards to a straight or flush with cards to come, as opposed to a *complete hand.*

draw out: Beat someone's hand by drawing.

early position: The first few positions to the left of the dealer, or to the left of the blinds.

extra outs: Cards that improve a hand in more ways than the self-evident *outs.*

family pot: A pot with a lot of players, sometimes as many as all at the table.

flop: The three *community cards* turned face up after the first round of betting.

free card: The situation in which there is no bet on a particular round, so players get extra cards without having had to risk additional money.

gut-shot: The card that makes an *inside straight,* or, more commonly, the making of a straight by catching a card *inside.*

hold'em: A form of poker with two cards dealt face down to each player, and five community cards dealt face up in the center of the table.

hole card: Any one of the *downcards.*

house: A cardroom or casino, or the management of a cardroom or casino; often preceded by *the.*

implied odds: The ratio of what you should win (including money likely to be bet in subsequent rounds) on a particular hand to what the current bet costs.

kicker: The unpaired card (side card) that goes with a player's pair or set. For example, a player with A-K and a board of K-9-2 has a pair of kings with an ace kicker (something known as top pair, top kicker).

kicker trouble: The situation in which you have a pair, but if someone else has the same pair, he likely has a higher kicker.

late position: Positions to the right of the dealer, that is, those that make their decisions after the first few players have acted.

leave money on the table: Fail to extract as much as possible (by not betting with what is almost certainly the best hand).

limp: Open for the limit in a *structured limit* game, as opposed to coming in for a raise.

live one: A very loose player, usually implying one who loses.

maniac: Someone who bets and raises wildly and at every possible opportunity — with little correlation to the value of his cards.

middle pair: The situation in which a player pairs one of his hole cards with something other than the highest card on the board.

middle position: Somewhere between early position and late position.

miracle: When poker players use this word, they generally mean the catching of a longshot, as, say, an inside straight or a third deuce when the player holds 2-2 against a higher pair.

muck: The *discards.*

nut: The best possible hand for the situation. Thus a *nut flush* is the best possible flush that can be made. With four hearts on the board, for example, whoever holds the A♡ has the nut flush. Similarly, with a board of 6♡ 7◇ 8◇ Q♡ A♣, anyone with hole cards T-9 of any suits would have the *nut straight.* That hand would also be known as *the nuts,* because it is the best possible hand that can be made with that board.

odds: The likelihood or unlikelihood of a particular event, usually expressed in the form of one number *to* a number.

offsuit: Descriptive of the hole cards being of different suits, as opposed to *suited.*

one gap: Describing starting cards in which the two cards are two apart in rank.

on the button: In the *button* position.

option: When the action is on the player who put in the *big blind,* and the pot has been opened for the minimum (that is, there has been no raise), that player may, if he wishes, raise. A house dealer may say "Your option," as a reminder.

outkicked: Losing with a pair because an opponent has the same pair, but with a higher kicker (side card). For example, you have J-T and the board is J-9-6-3-2. If you lose to a player with A-J, you have been *outkicked.*

outs: Cards that improve a hand, usually used with reference to a hand that is not currently the best hand.

overcard: A card on the board higher than the rank of your pair.

overcards: Cards higher than your pair, or cards higher than any on the board.

overlay: Receiving a better return than the pot odds indicate. For example, if the odds against making your hand are 2-to-1 and the pot offers 9-to-1, your hand is an overlay.

overpair: A player's pair higher than any card among the community cards.

pat hand: Complete, or five-card, hand, that is, a straight or better.

pocket pair: A pair as one's first two cards.

position: Where a player sits in relation to the dealer.

pot odds: The ratio of the size of the pot compared to the size of the bet a player must call to continue in the hand.

rag: A card in the flop that probably doesn't help players who started with good cards.

rainbow: Of all different suits.

rake: Take a percentage of the pot, usually by the *house* as its means of making money on the game.

ram and jam: Bet and raise frequently and aggressively.

read a hand: Make a conclusion about another player's holdings based on that player's actions, remarks, betting patterns, etc., and on the constitution of the board with relation to the preceding.

river: The fifth and final community card.

rock: An extremely tight player, one who takes few chances.

runner-runner: Flush or straight cards that arrive on the fourth and fifth cards, appearing for someone who, on the flop, had only three to that particular hand.

scare card: A scary-looking card for the situation. When two of one suit are on the board, the appearance of a third card of that suit may be a scare card for anyone for whom that card does not make a flush. If you had two pair when there were three spades on the board, you might worry about someone having the needed two spades with which to make the flush. And if the third of a suit is a scare card, the fourth suited card is even more so.

second pair: Forming a pair that consists of one of your hole cards matching the second-highest card on the board.

semibluff: A bet made on a hand that is probably not the best at the time of the bet, but that has two ways to win: either by getting everyone else to fold or, if called, that might improve on succeeding cards.

set: Three of a kind. To *flop a set* means that (most often) one started with a pair and one of those cards was among the flop.

showdown: The point in a hand, after all the betting is over, at which the players turn their cards face up for comparison with all active hands, to determine which hand wins the pot.

side pot: An auxiliary pot generated when one or more players run out of chips, and which those who ran out cannot win.

slow-play: Opting to not bet or raise with a good hand in the hope of trapping other players on this or subsequent rounds.

small blind: The player to the immediate left of the button puts chips into the pot equal to half the size of the lower limit of the game. Those chips (and the player who puts the chips in) are called the *small blind.*

smooth call: Call, and specifically not raise, on your turn.

solid: Conservative, not likely to get out of line; said of someone's play or a player.

steal position: In a game with blinds, a late position, often the *cutoff* (position one to the right of the button) or button; so used because it is most likely from this position that a player attempts to steal the blinds, that is, open with a raise in the hope of not getting called by either blind.

structured limit: Describing the betting structure of a limit game (as opposed to no-limit), that is, with bets at one level before and on the flop, and twice that level on the turn and river, such as $15-$30 hold'em.

suited: Descriptive of the first two cards being of the same suit, as opposed to *offsuit.*

tell: A mannerism that gives away your holdings.

Texas hold'em: The "official" name for hold'em.

the nuts: The best possible hand at a given point in a pot. See *nut.*

third pair: Forming a pair that consists of one of your hole cards matching the third-highest card on the board.

tight: Playing very conservatively; showing little gamble; not likely to take a chance; having stringent playing requirements.

tilt: The state of playing poorly and irrationally due to emotional upset, often caused by the player in question having had a good hand beat by a freak draw from another player or the player having lost a pot because of his own bad play.

top pair: The situation in which a player pairs one of his hole cards with the highest card on the board.

turn: The fourth card dealt to the center. Also known as *fourth street.*

underpair: A player's pair lower than any card among the community cards.

Some of the definitions in this glossary have been adapted from *The Official Dictionary of Poker* (©2005 Michael Wiesenberg) and are used with permission.